THE
UNKNOWN
AMBASSADORS

A Saga of Citizenship

Phyllis Michaux

THE UNKNOWN AMBASSADORS

A Saga of Citizenship

Phyllis Michaux

ALETHEIA
Publications

Michaux, Phyllis
The unknown ambassadors : a saga of citizenship /
Phyllis Michaux

Copyright © 1996 by Phyllis Michaux

Library of Congress Catalog Card Number: 95-83659
ISBN: 0-9639260-2-0

Copyeditor: John Matthews
Cover design: Guy J. Smith
Interior design and composition: Guy J. Smith
Cover photos: Front—Grassroots action by overseas
    voters (from left: Sonja Mincbere, Phyllis Michaux,
    Eloise Kriveoshia); back—photo of Phyllis Michaux
    by Lana Alexander Murawiec

Aletheia Publications
38-15 Corporal Kennedy St.
Bayside, NY 11361

Printed in Canada
10 9 8 7 6 5 4 3 2 1

Acknowledgments

I am indebted to all of those who have given their testimonials herein and allowed me to describe how their lives have been affected by U.S. laws applicable to overseas Americans. They are the heart and soul of this work.

I am especially grateful to Michael Adler, Kathleen and Jean Luc de Carbuccia, Alfred E. Davidson, Stephanie Simonard, and Andrew Sundberg for their invaluable support and friendship.

Other friends have contributed time and advice. Among them are Constance Borde, Gregory Good, Connie Helgue, Alice Jouve, Holly de Montmorin, Leo Packer, Dale Picot, Rhoda Seidler, Dorothy van Schooneveld, and Virginia Vittoz.

I thank my sister Carolyn Mitchell for her overall aid and Susan Shupard for her assistance with computer technology.

And finally my editor and publisher, Carolyn Smith, for her care and patience every step of the way.

CONTENTS

With her book, *The Unknown Ambassadors: A Saga of Citizenship,* Phyllis Michaux provides a unique and vivid journey through her experience as an "American abroad" and the constant challenges faced by this segment of our fellow U.S. citizens living in other countries. We are reminded that pride of citizenship is not a product of location, and we are inspired by her account to continue the battle against discrimination of all kinds.

—Senator John D. Rockefeller IV

Henriette: Do you consider it right to give up your country?

Ralph: Ah, one doesn't give up one's country any more than one gives up one's grandmother. They are both antecedent to choice—elements of one's composition that are not to be eliminated.

—Henry James,
Portrait of a Lady

Introduction

TODAY THERE are about 3 million Americans living abroad in 171 countries around the world. They are not very much in the public mind and are not generally recognized for the benefits they bring to America. They are the unknown ambassadors. Who are they? Americans have always traveled abroad, but before World War II such travel was usually restricted to the well-to-do, who took leisurely voyages on ocean liners and sent their children to Europe to "complete" their education. And for the most part, both parents and children returned to America and stayed. After World War II Europe experienced an influx of young Americans, mostly veterans on the GI Bill (among them Art Buchwald), but this group has received little attention. In contrast, the renown of American expatriates of the 1920s has remained alive and intact in American literature.

But although books continue to be written about Ernest Hemingway and Gertrude Stein, expatriates of this type are in fact long gone. These figures have been replaced by large numbers of middle-class Americans who reside overseas not for "the movable feast" but to earn their daily bread.

Attracted by the Marshall Plan reconstruction of Europe, these Americans began to cross the Atlantic in 1945.

Although the initial arrivals were federal government employees, businessmen quickly followed. Prewar commercial ties were reconstituted and expanded. Exporters, sales representatives, and manufacturers came to revitalize European larders and infrastructure. A whole range of products—from automobiles to pharmaceuticals, paper towels, and blue jeans—were produced and sold overseas. Safe under NATO's umbrella, other professions followed: engineers, bankers, lawyers, accountants, and advertisers. With the business community came students, teachers, artists, musicians, writers, missionaries, scientists, fashion models, and even professional basketball players. And they have been joined by increasing numbers of retirees.

In large European cities and elsewhere these Americans have created American communities with schools, libraries, churches, and nonprofit charitable and social associations. They bring with them American ways of doing things. They interact on a daily basis with the people of the host country, often a great deal more than do the members of the military and diplomatic corps.

In general, federal employees and members of the armed forces have their own installations, schools, and social groups. They are paid in American currency and have access to embassy cooperatives and military post exchanges that are not open to private U.S. citizens. This tends to divide overseas citizens into separate groups, especially in cities in which there is a large American community. Such differences between official and unofficial Americans would not necessarily hold true in countries where the number of American residents is small and the local culture very dissimilar to ours.

According to a 1994 State Department report, the largest American communities abroad are in Canada (422,000) and Mexico (463,500). In Europe, the greatest concentration of Americans is in London (200,000). There are 11,500 resident Americans in Edinburgh, Scotland, many of them employed by U.S. petroleum companies. Riyadh and Jeddah in Saudi Arabia together have 24,500. There are 44,000 Americans living in Tokyo, which is more than Paris's 25,000.

For the month of June 1995, Social Security benefits were paid outside the United States to 142,552 U.S. citizen beneficiaries. The Census Bureau makes no attempt to count private-sector overseas residents. Unofficial estimates of the total number of Americans living overseas run as high as 5 million, but nobody really knows. The State Department keeps track of how many passports are issued, but it cannot determine how many are no longer in use. There is no requirement for turning in an expired passport, nor is there any way of ascertaining where the bearer is residing when the passport expires. Registration at consular offices overseas is strongly recommended by the State Department, but many people do not comply.

Host country governments are not much better informed. Most of them undoubtedly keep records of the number of permits issued to foreigners authorized to reside in their country, but while they may know the number of residence permits issued, they have no way to determine how many Americans continue to live in the country once the permit has run its course or how many leave without making any formal declaration of departure.

Some overseas Americans are permanent residents of one country. Others may reside outside the United States for long periods but move from one country to another. A certain continuity is often maintained, however, because they stay with the same employer or at least remain active in the same field. Such is the case for State Department personnel as well as for those employed by foreign subsidiaries of American firms. However, all of these long-term overseas residents return to the United States to visit on a regular basis. Still others may live overseas for two to three years and then go back to the States and never again venture beyond its shores.

Certain overseas Americans are viewed by those at home as part of a well-defined entity with a worthwhile and steady purpose that requires overseas residence: military personnel and federal employees. The former are usually referred to as being "in the army or navy" and the latter as "with the foreign service." At best, the rest of the

Americans resident overseas "have gone to work in such and such a country" and at worst are regarded as tax avoiders, living it up in the sunny climes of the Mediterranean or the Caribbean. A problem for this latter group is their unfavorable image, or even lack of image, for want of knowledge of their very existence. As a consequence, they are often regarded with mistrust. There is widespread suspicion that Americans who leave the United States will no longer think of themselves as Americans. It is commonly assumed that prolonged residence in a foreign land will water down their feelings for home. Conforming to foreign manners will result in the loss of American ways, a kind of seepage from the inner core.

This distorted impression of overseas Americans confuses public officials—both those who make the laws and those who administer them—as they have no real picture of what Americans are doing overseas. This confusion is reflected in Congress and unfairly influences legislation affecting those living abroad.

Over the past thirty years, therefore, diverse groups of overseas citizens have engaged in efforts to change federal laws and regulations unfavorable to them. These provisions are primarily in the areas of voting rights, Medicare and other social benefits, citizenship laws, and taxation. Little by little, dedicated individuals and organizations have chipped away at discriminatory legislation in a struggle that has been largely ignored or poorly understood by their fellow Americans at home.

These efforts, which have extended over more than twenty years, have been almost totally successful in removing impediments to American citizenship for children born of American parents overseas.

Another area in which overseas Americans have worked successfully for change is voting registration. Procedures set up by state legislatures rendered absentee voting by overseas citizens very difficult and often impossible. A breakthrough came in 1975 with the passage of the Overseas Citizens Absentee Voting Rights Act, which facilitated absentee voting through a unified federal registration system. Since then, legislators—always sensitive to votes—have become somewhat more attentive to the problems of overseas Americans.

Although legislation to extend Medicare benefits to eligible U.S. citizens residing or simply traveling overseas was passed by the House (398–2) in 1978, a House-Senate reconciliation bill was dropped from consideration in 1980. Another unfair practice is the discontinuation of Supplemental Security Income payments to Americans when they go to live abroad. This is particularly unjust to American parents of a handicapped child; when they are posted to a foreign country, that support is lost.

Contrary to popular belief, U.S. citizens overseas *do* pay taxes. They are liable both to the American government and to that of the country where they reside. Although a foreign tax credit is available, this does not take into account the heavy value-added sales taxes imposed by some foreign governments or the cost and complication of preparing returns for the Internal Revenue Service. The United States is the only industrialized nation in the world that taxes its overseas citizens on income earned abroad from foreign sources.

Most of the efforts to correct these inequities have been carried out by American organizations in Europe. This book presents an account of those endeavors, in which I participated between 1961 and 1995. Although it is a personal story, it has been written for overseas Americans themselves and for those who were and those who still are active in campaigns to secure and protect their rights as American citizens. This informal summary tries to bind all of the threads together so as to form a historical record.

But this book also seeks a wider audience. It attempts to describe Americans resident overseas to their fellow citizens at home. I hope that it will correct some misimpressions and lead the way to a more realistic view of these Americans so that eventually this "overseas corps" will receive the support and recognition it deserves.

An American in Paris

MY LIFE as an overseas American began in 1946 when I
fell in love with a Frenchman. We had met in New York
through mutual friends. Employed in a family business,
he had come to America to renew commercial ties inter-
rupted by the long war years. I had left Paris only a year
before, returning to Fort Dix, New Jersey, to be discharged
from the U.S. Army. Eighteen months of my service—from
1943 to 1945—had been spent in the European theater of
operations in London, Paris, and Wiesbaden.

I returned to Paris in November 1946, this time to be
married. Then and there I had my first encounter with American citizenship laws. The wedding was all organized and
the paperwork had been completed according to French law
and the customs of the day, with both a civil and a religious
ceremony. A reception would be held at the Hotel George V.
At the last minute, thinking of an amendment to my passport to add the change in name, I stopped by the American
Embassy. It was a Thursday afternoon. There I faced Agnes
Schneider, head of the passport office. She was a strong-
featured woman with an aura of authority visible to the
naked eye. Totally unprepared and with no idea that
Schneider was already a legend in the small American community of that time, I gaily outlined my plans for the wedding to be held the following Monday.

She responded in an absolute tone of voice: "If you marry that Frenchman on Monday, I will take away your passport!" Or did she say, "You will lose your citizenship"? No matter; to me the threat was clear. My consternation would have been about the same had she pronounced the impending amputation of an arm or leg. My citizenship! It was just not possible—not within any realm of reality. Not once in my life had I even thought about my citizenship; it just *was*. My citizenship defined an inherent characteristic of myself, as in "My hair is brown; my eyes are green; I am an American." I received a strong shock with afterwaves that remain to this day and are rendered concrete and visible with this book.

Schneider went on to explain that French law regulating marriage by a French citizen to an alien had changed six weeks before. The marriage automatically conferred French citizenship on a foreign spouse unless it was formally rejected prior to the ceremony. U.S. law did not allow the acquisition of a second nationality, for which the immediate retribution was loss of American citizenship.

The solution, she said, was to prepare a declaration renouncing the offer of French citizenship, which would have to be signed before a notary and submitted in the required number of copies to French authorities. This meant more trips to city hall, which we set out to do in record time.

Had Schneider declared *her* interpretation of U.S. law or that of her superiors in Washington in insisting that the passive acquisition of French citizenship constituted "obtaining naturalization in a foreign state upon his own application," for which the "sentence" was loss of U.S. citizenship?[1]

My husband and I managed to conclude the paperwork in time. My passport was still mine, but a real feeling of insecurity remained. Henceforth, I regarded the embassy with apprehension at passport renewal time. I was anxious to fill out the forms correctly, to give the right answers to the questions of consular officers, and fearful of a misstep with rules and regulations unknown to me.

The Case of Madame G

As I learned later, Schneider administered the law to the letter, without regard for the special circumstances of the war. Witness the case of Madame G., the American wife of a French citizen, who was unable to leave France before the occupation by German troops in 1940. With her husband a prisoner of war, she found herself alone with two young children. In order to avoid the internment camps to which so many Americans and other foreigners were consigned, she obtained false documents identifying her as a French citizen. When the war was over, Schneider refused to renew her American passport on the ground that Madame G. had voluntarily sought French citizenship. Madame G. lost not only her own U.S. citizenship but also that of her children.

There was another shocking case involving an American woman who had acquired French citizenship upon marriage. During the German occupation of France, both she and her husband had joined a Resistance group. Before she was caught by the Germans, she had successfully helped sixty downed Allied airmen make it to safety in Spain. She survived a nine-month stay in the horrible Ravensbruck concentration camp. After the war, the French government offered a monetary compensation more honorific than substantial to her and other resistants, which she accepted. Under a provision of an American law that said in substance that U.S. citizens who, upon acquiring a foreign nationality, take advantage of that nationality forfeit their citizenship, Schneider refused to issue her an American passport. However, the intervention of several high-ranking American army officers put a stop to Schneider's initiative that time. How did consular officers treat similar cases in other countries? There may be sad tales in State Department archives.

In the 1960s, when more friendly relations with the passport office had been established, a consular officer offered to set right the brutal rendering of the law and restore U.S. citizenship to Madame G. and to any others who had been ill treated. The consulate did not go so far as to seek out people listed in their own records. Perhaps their filing system did not lend itself to the project, not having a category for "iniquitous decisions." In any case, Madame G., still bitter, refused this tardy rectification.

Another proposal was accepted, however. Madame L. had forfeited her U.S. citizenship upon her marriage to a French citizen after World War I. As a widow approaching her seventh decade, it was obvious even to Washington bureaucrats that she could not possibly represent a threat to the security of the United States. The consulate issued her a new American passport, and she was overjoyed to receive it.

She had married before the passage of the Cable Act in 1922. Until then, American women (but not men) who married aliens were automatically divested of their birthright, even if both the woman and her alien husband made their home in America.

I later learned that many American women married Frenchmen in the United States, never thinking of advising either the French Consulate or any American official and thus unwittingly acquiring French citizenship. As long as they were residents of the United States, there was no problem, but some of them ran into difficulties when taking up residence in France. They were asked if they had acquired French citizenship upon marriage, and if so, had they used a French passport? Those who had been previously warned could lie and say no. But others in a happy state of ignorance said yes. What happened then? The answers I've heard have varied, for as time went by the attitudes of consular officers improved as a consequence of a more comprehensive view in Washington.

An Unwelcome Surprise

My daughter was born in Paris in 1949. Soon thereafter I took her to the embassy to register her birth as an

American citizen, and she was added to my passport with no particular difficulty. But only at that time was another section of the law explained to me. In order to retain her U.S. citizenship, she would have to complete five consecutive years of residence in the United States between the ages of fourteen and twenty-eight.

I could not help but feel resentful toward Schneider, who was still directing the passport office. She could have told me about this requirement at the time of our earlier encounter. I could have gone to my parents' home in New York and given birth in the United States, thereby assuring unconditional citizenship for my child. But she had told me nothing, and I had never asked. It did not occur to me to question her authority or to obtain a copy of the Immigration and Nationality Act and read the law for myself.

On the other hand, the State Department, through the consulate, certainly did nothing to inform Americans of the pitfalls in citizenship laws. It was not until the late 1970s that I saw a brochure published for the use of overseas citizens that set forth the provisions for the retention and loss of U.S. citizenship.

The formality of registering my daughter to my passport was carried out without my even becoming aware of the section of the law that allowed the transmission of citizenship from parent to child. At that time, an American parent resident overseas and married to a foreign spouse must have lived ten years in the United States prior to the birth of a child. Five of those years had to be after the age of fourteen.[2] This residence requirement for transmission has since been reduced to five years, two of which must be after the age of fourteen.

A Dual-Cultural Existence

During the 1950s, I was living within the financial limitations of a young married couple and devoting myself to my children and household. I existed in relative isolation from the American community, which was then much smaller and different from what it is today. There were some American organizations, however. Each month the American Women's Group in Paris held a formal luncheon. Decked out with a hat and gloves, I attended these meetings in the hope of making some friends. In those years most of the attendees were wives of U.S. Army and Air Force officers, NATO personnel, embassy staff, or the businessmen who were just beginning to arrive. The life of these women was free of any need for permanent adaptation and eased by things American—post exchanges (PX's), commissaries, and Department of Defense schools for their children were all available to them in France. They were like permanent tourists with all the trimmings. I could listen to what they said, but there was no common ground; our lives were too different.

My own contacts with America were restricted to letters and occasional visitors from home. Other than the monthly luncheons of the women's group, I rarely encountered other Americans. Getting a telephone call through to the States was a major event. It required a reservation of the time slot, which could take up to two or three days. Hearing the voices of family members brought forth all my homesickness for them and for my country. In the kitchen amid the fumes of boiling diapers, I would sometimes look at a little souvenir Eiffel Tower I kept on the stove and say to myself, "Cheer up! You are in Paris!"

It wasn't all rosy learning to live with the French either. Coming out of the five years of isolation imposed by the war while the world had moved along in all fields, they were anchored in 1939 instead of the mid-1940s. Their limited knowledge of American customs and my insufficient French vocabulary made for frequent misinterpretations. Describing the occupation of my father, a lawyer who held a worthy position in the U.S. Treasury Department, was very difficult. Knowing nothing of French government administration, I could not define a counterpart occupation. This tended to convince my mother-in-law that I had married her son for money. Once a letter from my mother announced that my young sister had earned five dollars babysitting. My father-in-law was shocked. "What is this! Your sister works?" In spite of the explanations of my husband, who knew America well, it was only years later that an American movie (*Mr. Belvedere*, featuring Clifton Webb as a babysitter) made the situation clear to him. I learned to modify descriptions of my background and former life according to what I perceived to be their knowledge and experience. On my first trip home I spent much of my time explaining the French and France to Americans. When I returned, I continued to interpret American behavior to the French. The arrival of Coca-Cola was a good case in point: French women anxiously inquired about the consequences of giving it to their children.

It was a different world in the 1950s, as illustrated by the following quote from *Americans Abroad: Two Centuries of European Travel:*

> Within a decade of the war's end, a busy day at New York's International Airport at Idlewild might see as many as fifty planes, each one carrying as many as seventy-five passengers, heading out over the Atlantic on flights that overnight carried them to Europe's major cities.[3]

The first jets were introduced for commercial flights in 1958. Up until then, Paris–New York flights were made on four-engine Constellations. With refueling stops in Shannon, Ireland, and Gander, Newfoundland, the trip took eighteen hours or more.

There were no European editions of American magazines. The *New York Herald Tribune*, published in Paris, became very important to me, doubling as a mental security blanket. There was no television, of course, but there were American films in their original English versions showing on the Champs-Elysées.

I spoke English to my children and they spoke English to me. They spoke French with their father and his family. Up to about the age of five and six, they were bilingual with French dominant. They learned English simply by using it. If asked during a meal to pass the butter, for example, they would do so with no problem. But if asked to give the French word for butter, there was a hesitation, as if there were two separate language tracks, each with its own memory bank and set of reference terms.

This informal way of handling the two languages worked very well until the autumn of 1955. After a four-month summer stay with my family in Washington, my son, then five years old, forgot French. He gave it up completely. After we returned to Paris, school began before his French returned from wherever knowledge of languages goes under such conditions. He began to stutter, and to make things worse, he was teased by other children. What to do? There was no real advice to be had anywhere—no Dr. Spock-type book with a chapter on unavoidable bilingualism. There were no counselors for parents raising children with two maternal languages. All opinions differed. Finally we concluded that perfecting his English at a later date would be easier than correcting an ingrained speech problem. We became a French-language-only household.

About this time my passport was due for renewal. As it carried my son as well, he came with me to the embassy. By that time he was so mixed up that he refused to respond or even react when spoken to in English. I spoke French to him, curbing his explorations around the consular officer's desk and filing cabinets. The young official was obviously displeased with this American mother who had not taught English to her child. I explained the situation, but he didn't seem very convinced. Through no one's fault what might have been a pleasant situation became awkward.

And the basic problem remained: My husband and I needed to know how to raise our children so they would have equal ability in both languages. We wished to prepare them to span the Atlantic, to take advantage of their dual-cultural background. We wondered how other French-American families were coping with this same predicament.

These questions and others, along with my general uncertainty with regard to my children's American citizenship, were finally addressed by the establishment of the Association of American Wives of Europeans in 1961.

Notes

1. See Appendix B for the text of the law.
2. See Appendix B.
3. Rhea Foster Dulles, *Americans Abroad: Two Centuries of European Travel* (Ann Arbor: University of Michigan Press, 1964), p. 174.

2

We Get Organized
(1961–1968)

IN 1961 I met Mary D., another American woman with a French husband, and we became friends. It was a joy to be able to discuss, compare, and analyze our occasional resentment with life in France. For Mary, dealing with two languages and passing on her American background to her children had presented problems similar to mine.

Considering that we were in a fashion immigrants to France, we compared ourselves with war brides in the United States, wondering how Japanese and German women fared there. Were they quickly absorbed into new lives as first-generation Americans, detaching themselves from the language and culture of their homeland? Did they insist on speaking in their own language to their children? If so, did they use that language at home *and* in public? Arriving from countries that had been enemies of America, were they less inclined than we to strive to imprint their own culture on their children? Was it easier for us in France as citizens of the country whose soldiers had won the war? Was it due to some implacable characteristic of American women that we felt so strongly about raising our children not only to *be* but to *feel* American?

And what of the children themselves? If they were educated to the full extent of both parents' cultural backgrounds, they would become bilingual and bicultural adults. Whether they followed careers in international business or government, they would be especially suited to contribute to improved understanding between nations. In the meantime, we were wondering whether our children would even be allowed to keep their U.S. citizenship. It had been granted when they were registered at the American Embassy shortly after birth. But under section 301 (b) of the Immigration and Nationality Act of 1960, as children born overseas of one American parent they would lose their American citizenship unless they lived five consecutive years in the United States between the ages of fourteen and twenty-eight. This meant that they had to move to the United States at some point before their twenty-third birthday, and they could leave the country for only thirty days each year.[1]

The law made no distinction as to whether the American parent was the mother or the father. However, there was a very practical advantage for an American father, who was likely to be an overseas employee of an American company. Home leave and tours of duty in the States would make it easier for his children to fulfill the required residence period. The foreign spouse would probably reside in the United States at some point and become a naturalized citizen. In 1960, only three years of residence in the United States were required for the naturalization of a foreign spouse. Once the spouse had acquired American citizenship, any child of theirs born abroad would be born of two American citizen parents and would be subject to a different section of the law. Such citizen-parents faced a residence requirement so minimal that it posed no problem whatsoever. Arranging for the birth of a child in the United States was also facilitated by employment with an American firm. Once again, home leave, a tour of duty in the States, and the financial advantage of having American medical insurance all helped to ease the way to citizenship with no restrictions.

We were not dismayed, however. Totally ignorant of the actual workings of the legislative process, we really believed that if Congress could be made to recognize that these young people would grow up able to work and live with ease on both sides of the Atlantic, changes in the law would inevitably follow. Our government would recognize their potential value and, ceasing to reject them, welcome them as valuable elements of the postwar generation.

Initial Efforts

Mary's three children and my two were all under twelve. It seemed as if we had enough time to undertake some action, although we had no idea what form it might take. We could carry out the first step, which was to seek out other American women married to French men.

With the idea of gathering some statistics on the numbers of international couples and their offspring, we drafted a questionnaire that included questions on numbers of children, places of birth, professions of wives and husbands, and the language ability of both parents and children. Along with three other American women Mary knew, we called a meeting and placed an ad in the *New York Herald Tribune* that read,

> American wives of Frenchmen resident in France are invited to a meeting to be held on April 26 at 3 PM, 65 Quai d'Orsay to discuss problems specific to them, among others their civil rights.

The American Church on the Quai d'Orsay let us use a pleasant meeting room. It was furnished with several black leather couches, comfortable chairs, and miscellaneous tables; the windows overlooked the Seine. Standing at one end behind a table, text in hand and trembling inside, I addressed the small group of fifteen women who showed up. In part, I said,

> We, American women residing abroad and married to foreign citizens, should be considered an asset by our country. If there is ever going to be one world, and we all hope the United States will lead it, we are in a certain sense its pioneers. The attitude of some U.S. consular officials seems to

imply that we are second-class citizens. Entering into the state of matrimony has nothing whatsoever to do with one's loyalty to one's country. Moreover, it can safely be assumed that we marry into the pro-American element of any given population.

Turning to the issue of citizenship laws, I explained my belief that if we had an opportunity to show Congress that our bicultural children had the potential to make a valuable contribution to international affairs, there would surely be no difficulty in getting the residence clause removed from the law. No one questioned this notion. In retrospect, I wonder how we could have been so naive.

Further discussion focused on practical matters: summer charter flights to the States, gaining access to the post exchange located in the American Embassy, and possibilities for employment with the American Embassy and other American government missions to France. Why couldn't we be hired locally to fill the clerical positions held by French citizens? Other topics of discussion included methods of teaching English to our children and holding parties for them where they could meet other French-American youngsters.

Several of the women left before the end of the meeting, but those who stayed agreed that the first step was to form an organization so that together we could work to improve our situation.

Vivienne Fortier was one of those who stayed. Born and raised in New York City, she had joined the U.S. Army as a dietitian. In 1944 she was in Paris in the Lycée Claude Bernard, a high school that had been transformed into a hospital for American troops. She had married a French citizen shortly after the war and had two children. She volunteered to handle funds.

Another addition to our small group was Gertrude de Gallaix. Originally from Chicago, Gertrude had married a French lawyer just before World War II. She had lived through the German occupation of France only to be widowed shortly after the liberation. She continued to live in France, becoming a professional translator specializing in legal documents. Over the years she translated hundreds of contracts and agreements between French and American firms and individuals. Proficient in explaining the subtle meanings of words and phrases, she was one of the little-known links in the postwar renewal of commercial ties between France and America.

Gertrude's primary interest was in women's organizations both within and outside the Paris community. One of these, the Federation of American Women's Clubs Overseas (FAWCO), was meeting in The Hague in May. Founded in 1932, this umbrella organization had fifteen member clubs based in European capitals, plus two in Saudi Arabia. The keynote speaker at the conference was to be the wife of General Lauris Norstad, Commander of American military forces in Europe. Gertrude, who would be attending the conference as a delegate of the Paris American Women's Group, volunteered to raise the subject of U.S. citizenship laws. Glad of the opportunity to extend our survey to other American communities, we gave her copies of our questionnaire to distribute.

Among the resolutions voted at that conference was one of special interest to us: recommend that FAWCO study the question of United States citizenship status with emphasis on the problems confronting persons born abroad of a U.S. citizen and a non-U.S. citizen, and seek, if desirable, ways in which pertinent legislation can be initiated or supported.

FAWCO also established a citizenship committee, headed by a member of the American Women's Group of Rome.

Shortly thereafter my husband went to Rome on business and I tagged along. I was able to meet with some of the the American women of that club. The members married to Italians with children born in Italy knew exactly what I was driving at. They responded by forming a committee within the Rome club that would be devoted to the same goals as ours in Paris.

Our group in Paris met twice more before breaking up for summer vacation, each time gaining in numbers.

There was no need for another ad in the *Tribune*—the grapevine was operating.

First Contacts with the Powers That Be

During my summer trip home to Washington I was able to meet with the head of the French Desk of the United States Information Agency (USIA). My first question was about employment with the American Embassy in Paris. He confirmed that it was State Department policy not to hire American citizens locally. He believed that the policy had begun immediately after the surrender of Germany on May 8, 1945. Very few American civilians were living in Paris at that time and those who were had probably lived through the German occupation and were still putting their lives together again. As a consequence, the State Department and other federal agencies hired English-speaking French citizens. This practice continued in the postwar years despite the existence of an ever-growing American community in Paris.

Proceeding to more immediate goals, I explained that our group would be formally organized in the fall. It would be important for us to have some recognition from the American Embassy. I asked that he inform the appropriate State Department office of our existence and purpose.

He put me in touch with the women's activities advisor for the USIA, who happened to be the wife of Carl Marcy, the chief of staff of the Senate Foreign Relations Committee. She listened to what I had to say and then passed me along to the president of the Foreign Service Wives Association and finally to an assistant secretary of state for education and cultural affairs.

These were my first meetings in official Washington. There have been many others over the years. For the most part federal employees have been cooperative and helpful. Results have not always been positive and certainly not rapid, but in general, career civil-service people will make themselves available. They will give you their time and attention. This accessibility is among the greatest forces of our democratic system and one that may not be fully appreciated by people who have never lived outside the United States.

The Association of American Wives of Europeans

In September our fledgling organization met again and gave itself a name: The Association of American Wives of Europeans (AAWE). Hebe Dorsey, a veteran reporter for the *Tribune*, attended our October meeting. Her article—"Americans with French Husbands"—included my telephone number. The phone started ringing and didn't stop for days. Finally I set aside Thursday afternoons to receive visits from those who had called. Some of them were leading very isolated lives, just as I had ten years before. It was evident that most of these young women were just plain lonely. They were glad of an opportunity to talk about their lives, their children, domestic problems, travel to America, and their adaptation to French ways.

The Dorsey article drew the attention of David Schoenbrun, who then headed the CBS office in Paris. He decided that our first Halloween party was a suitable event for television. The party was held in my home in Auteuil. The living room had been made as festive as possible, and the dozen or so children were dressed in costumes. Schoenbrun interviewed several of the mothers, asking how and where they had met their husbands and about their impressions of France. He cautioned us that the material he was filming would not necessarily appear on American television screens. He was right. The story was dropped in favor of another about Caroline Kennedy.

By November our group consisted of fifty to sixty women. The first and most important task was for them to meet and get to know one another. Betsy K., an energetic let's-get-moving type of person, placed colored pins on a map of Paris to represent where each person lived. She then organized afternoon teas according to the clusters of pins that had appeared on the map—a very effective method. Soon the women were exchanging information about their neighborhoods and walking out together with their children. They had found someone to talk to, someone to partially replace their friends and family left behind in America. It soon became clear that most of them had met their husbands while in college: either the American wife had studied in France or the husband had attended an American university. It was a talented and well-educated group, and a surprising number of these original members have remained active to this day.[2]

In July 1962, several AAWE members and I met with consular officer Larry Winter Roeder. We described the aims of the AAWE, stressing our efforts to impart our background and language to our children. We expressed our concerns about the citizenship laws—not only with the requirement of five years' continuous residence, but also the section requiring ten years' prior residence in the United States for the American parent (with a foreign spouse) to transmit citizenship in the first place. Several women had come to us after their newborn infants had been denied U.S. citizenship. For example, one young mother's family had spent a year in Canada when she was in her teens. As a result, she had not resided in the United States for the full required ten years. This seemed to be a most unfair requirement, since children go where and when their parents take them. She had been caught unawares and learned of the requirement only when she had gone to the passport office to register her child as an American citizen. Seeing that the father was a French citizen, the consular officer asked her how long she had lived in the United States prior to the birth of the child. When she counted her years of residence she came up four months short. The consular officer refused to register the baby as a U.S. citizen.

How were those ten years counted, we asked? What constituted proof of residence—school records, driver's licenses, affidavits from family and friends? Why couldn't Americans be informed of these laws when they applied for a passport in the United States or abroad? In fact, why couldn't a brief reference to these stipulations be added to the passport itself? In this manner, everyone who went overseas or who was already overseas would be fully informed. How could we obtain the exact wording of the law in order to copy it and distribute it to our members? Roeder was very cooperative and offered to come to a panel discussion on citizenship laws. But first he asked that AAWE members submit written questions, which would be sent on to Frances Knight, then head of the passport office in Washington. When the answers were received, he would preside at a question-and-answer session for our members. He also informed us that the consulate had begun to issue birth certificates. This was important news that was soon published in our newsletter.

The meeting with Roeder was held the following January. To the best of my knowledge this was the first time, at least in France, that the consulate had used the channels of a local organization to advise American citizens of changes in laws and regulations affecting them. Roeder gave me his own copy of the Immigration and Nationality Act. I was very touched and used it to commit "our" sections to memory. I cited and recited them upon every occasion whether it was timely or not. I had turned into a woman with a cause.

Since that meeting every member of the AAWE has been kept informed of U.S. citizenship laws through our newsletter and by way of special reports. As a rule, the chairman and members of the citizenship committee have dispensed advice and counsel on special situations to members and nonmembers alike.

During these early years, I made an effort to make AAWE known to American and French-American organizations within the American community. My husband and I began to attend social functions that we had hitherto ignored. Once, at a formal dinner of the Club France-Amérique, I met Henri Bonnet, the well-loved postwar French ambassador to the United States. By then I had developed a four-sentence, one-minute spiel promoting the AAWE. Bonnet listened to me with great courtesy and agreed to be the guest of honor at one of our luncheons.

Satisfied, I moved on. Later in the evening I heard my name called and turned to see him waving from the doorway as he left. His voice silenced the large reception room: "Tenez-moi au courant" (Keep me informed). It was a wonderful moment.

Addressing Bilingualism

Shortly thereafter we held our first meeting on bilingualism, inviting Ruth W. Metraux, a psychologist with the United Nations Educational, Scientific, and Cultural Organization (UNESCO), to give us some much-needed practical advice. She then turned the coin by undertaking a study of our members. Her study centered on twenty-five French-American families and asked only two questions: "Give a short history of how your children learned two languages," and "Have there been any problems along the way? If so, how did you resolve them?" Her report was published in the *French Review* in April 1965. In the summary, she noted that the degree of education of both parents in the participating families was considerably higher than that of the average person in either France or the United States and that the socioeconomic background of those families, as indicated by the occupation of the fathers, was well above average. The parents listed a variety of teaching methods, including the following: all bedtime, eating, bathing, and dressing routines were carried out in English; they used sing-song pronunciation games to ensure that their children learned how to pronounce the *th* and *r* sounds in English; the mother spoke only English to the children and never replied if they spoke French to her (the father did the same with French); and a child learning how to write in French at school was taught how to write in English by the mother at home. Any opportunity to get their children to hear and speak the English language was used, such as hiring American or English students to care for the children after school and providing English-language books, games, and recordings. Children were sent to England for short school vacations when they were old enough and of course to America itself for longer stays. The visits of family members and friends from America were very beneficial. Thus began a series of meetings, panel discussions, and conferences designed to assist and support parents who wished their children to be equally fluent in both French and English.

The members of AAWE have consistently followed through on these initial efforts. There is still a children's committee that organizes play groups in neighborhoods and hosts celebrations of American holidays. Putting preschoolers in contact with other children who speak English and linking their mothers with other mothers who speak French with an American accent has had very positive results. For young children the outside world becomes similar to the one at home where two languages are spoken. For older children, there may be special reading classes and informal instruction in American history to supplement the education given in French schools. Some of these youngsters switch with ease between French and English, speaking both languages without any discernible accent. Many are enrolled in private bilingual schools where instruction is given in both languages. But most attend the excellent public school system, where all pupils begin to learn a foreign language, usually English, at age twelve. It may happen that some are so competent in English that they may elect to learn any of the other languages taught in French high schools; as a result, upon completion of secondary school they may call themselves trilingual.

In November 1975, as an outgrowth of various studies and panel discussions held over the preceding twelve years, AAWE published its *Guidelines on Bilingualism*. This publication is explicitly concerned with French-American children, but its conclusions are of value for all bicultural children. It is equally useful to families in which three languages are spoken—those of each of the parents as well as that of the country of residence. The text presents an analysis of language use in the home and in school. Advice is given on dealing with a child's rejection of a language and handling visits by family members from America, who often do not speak the language of the country of residence. There is a very special frustration for grandparents who cannot communicate with their grandchildren.[3]

Addressing College Attendance

Shortly after its founding, AAWE began to look into college scholarships for dual nationals. Gaining a university degree in the United States would offer a solution to two problems. First, the young person would have a chance to live in the United States in order to fulfill the required residence period. Second, a completion and a pulling together of the two educational systems would prepare the dual national to live and work in either Europe or the United States or, for that matter, anywhere in the world. We set up yet another committee, calling it the AAWE Scholarship Program for Dual National Students. In December 1963 a letter was sent to 400 American universities, foundations, and educators setting forth the problems and the catch-22 dilemmas faced by the dual national student. Often these students are ineligible for financial aid in the United States. Because they are not residents of any state, they cannot apply for aid when it is given on a regional-residence basis. Yet they are not eligible for aid given exclusively to foreign students because they are not foreign.

In 1977 Olive Lorsignol, chair of the education committee, went to the States for her twenty-fifth reunion at Smith College. While there she visited nineteen colleges to acquaint them with American dual national students and the particular problems and advantages such students would present.

These personal contacts helped to clear up questions on citizenship status, the admission process, tests, forms, and placement policy. Among other things, Lorsignol explained the problems of academic equivalence, the transfer of credits between American and European institutions, and how applications for admission and financial aid might be facilitated. One immediate result of her visit was the creation of a scholarship for a young dual national student at Sweetbriar College. It is still in effect today.

It seems incredible now that so little information was available to American parents overseas to help them prepare their children for college admissions. Responding to that need, in 1994 the AAWE in collaboration with the École Active Bilingue (JM) began a series of annual meetings called "College Days." Guidance counselors, parents, and representatives of French-American groups brought together more than sixty representatives of well-known American colleges and universities. Parents and students were able to meet with those representatives, ask questions, obtain documentation, and receive briefings on the application process. The French office of the Fulbright program (the Franco-American Commission for Educational Exchange) takes an active part in these exchanges.

AAWE Today

As with more traditional women's clubs, AAWE conducts a number of charitable functions. The annual Christmas Bazaar clears enough money to make donations to both French and American organizations, including a Ronald McDonald House that houses the families of young cancer victims being treated at Villejuif, the French National Center for Cancer Research (CNRS).

The October 1994 AAWE newsletter announced the following events for the month: a children's Halloween party, presentation of an AAWE scholarship winner, a PSAT test, a panel on basic bilingualism, a seminar on wills and inheritance in France, and a family picnic and baseball game. The newsletter also announced three special reports. One is an update of an 1980 survey titled *College Education in the United States as Experienced by Dual Nationals*. The second is about reentry into the French higher education system after study in the United States.

The last publication, *Grown-Up Children of French-American Families in France*, is a report on ongoing research conducted by Gabrielle Varro, a sociologist at the CNRS and the author of books on American women and their children's bilingualism.[4] The new study contains information gathered by questionnaire in 1991 for four generations ranging from the AAWE members' own parents and parents-in-law to their grandchildren. It reveals the grown-up children's linguistic, academic, professional, and personal itineraries, including choices of spouse and country of residence. But above all, it seeks to investigate what happens to French-American culture when the second generation become parents—how they raise their own children linguistically and culturally. Do they continue to transmit the American language and culture that their parents worked so hard at keeping up? From first results, reported in an article titled "The Beginning and the Becoming of a 'Mixed' Culture," it would appear that not all of them continue to transmit English to their own children (a role they often leave to the grandmother). However, the education they received from their French fathers and American mothers and the attitudes and values learned at home doubtless persist in an "internationalized" identity. In-depth interviews with adult French-Americans should yield insights into what this type of cultural identity is made up of and what it means to them.

French-American marriages show no signs of tapering off. AAWE membership hovers between 500 and 600. Although only fourteen states are not represented, 47 percent of the members come from the East Coast of the United States. Eighty-three percent of the members have a bachelor's degree, 33 percent have a master's, and 6 percent have doctorates. Over half of the members are employed either full or part time as lawyers, teachers, journalists, secretaries, psychologists, education consultants, interpreters, translators, and small-business owners. As bilingual long-time residents, they are employed by both French and American business firms and nonprofit institutions. With a few exceptions, they were not eligible for local-hire positions with American embassies and consulates until the passage of the Rockefeller bill in 1991.[5]

In 1995 AAWE celebrated its thirty-fourth anniversary.

Notes

1. See Appendix B.

2. One of them is Harriet Frankel, who taught for some years at the American School of Paris. The bilingualism of her children was especially favored as her husband, employed by TWA, could offer his family frequent low-cost trips to America.

3. AAWE now publishes a *Guide to Education* aimed at the problems of all American families who are raising their children in France. It answers such questions as: Are you baffled by the French school system? Would you like your child to be bilingual? It contains equivalency charts for American, British, and French levels and lists forty-two bilingual French-English schools in Paris and its suburbs.

4. Gabrielle Varro, "Couples franco-américain en France: génèse et devenir d'une mixité," in *Mariages mixtes, Hommes et Migrations*, 1167 (July 1993), pp. 20-25; *The Transplanted Woman, A Study of French-American marriages in France* (New York: Praeger, 1988); *La Femme transplantée. Une étude du mariage franco-américain en France et le bilinguisme des enfants* (Presses Universitaires de Lille, 1984).

5. See Chapter 9.

Lose One, Win One
(1969–1972)

IN EARLY July of 1969, my mail contained a news item cut from the *Washington Post.* It came from a chance acquaintance with whom I had discussed our citizenship problems. Aged and often housebound, she called herself a "clipper." She selected, cut out, and sent newspaper articles to a miscellaneous group of people of varied interests. She is long gone now, but that kind and almost random gesture began a whole series of events.

Dated June 3, 1969, the article stated that in March of that year a federal court had ruled section 301 (b) of the Immigration and Nationality Act unconstitutional. This section defined the five-year required residence period for children born abroad of one American parent only. The ruling declared that the provision violated the Fifth Amendment's guarantee of due process of law. The case was scheduled to be taken up on appeal by the Supreme Court. The article continued,

> The judges said they were aware of the considerable danger that children born and reared abroad, schooled where English is not taught [and] celebrating foreign holidays with the family of the non-American parent, will have no meaningful connections with the United States, its culture, or [its] heritage.

To me this last sentence was astonishing and appalling. How could the judges themselves be so lacking in meaningful connnections with their own times? How could they not be aware of how far and in how many ways American culture had spread to other countries? Did they think their fellow citizens would completely turn their backs on the United States, to the point of not even speaking English to their own children? If such were the case, why would Americans overseas bother to register the birth of their children with an American embassy in the first place?

That the required residence period had been declared unconstitutional and would be struck from the law was wonderful news. But we sat back to await for the appeal.

The court had acted in the case of a twenty-nine-year-old Italian American named Aldo Bellei. The son of an American mother and an Italian father, he had been born and brought up in Italy. Although he had never resided in the United States, he had come to the States for visits and had registered for the draft. In 1964 the American Embassy in Rome had refused to issue him a new passport because he had not complied with the residence requirement. In such cases citizenship was considered to be forfeited at age twenty-three as that was the last point at which the five-year residence period could begin in order to be completed by age twenty-eight.

A second clipping from the *Washington Post,* dated July 8, 1969, brought word that the Immigration and Naturalization Service (INS), with some twenty-five related cases under active consideration and several hundred others pending, would appeal the decision to the Supreme Court. It also gave the name of Aldo Bellei's lawyer, O. John Rogge of Weisman, Celler, Allan, Spett & Sheinberg, a New York firm. This was the opportunity we had been waiting for.

On August 28, I wrote to Mr. Rogge describing our group and asking how we might help. I explained that we had observed that compliance with the law was largely dependent on one's finances. Those who had enough money gave birth to their children in the United States, thereby avoiding any problems associated with residence requirements for retention of U.S. citizenship. The children of parents who could not, for whatever reason, return to the United States for this purpose received this conditional citizenship. To a large extent, the same consideration held true for the five-year residence requirement itself. Those who were able to do so sent their children to college in the United States. I also explained our children's programs, stating that they were designed

> to give them all we can of their American background and heritage, allowing them to develop at a very early age an emotional attachment, the knowledge that America is their country. Thus, we prepared them to be at home and gain their livelihood in both countries, France and America.

Rogge answered promptly and informed us that the Supreme Court would probably hear the case. He believed that our best course of action would be to file an *amicus curiae* or friend of the court brief; it could be filed on behalf of many people and stress the points I had raised in my letter.

In October the Court granted review of the case. Then the real work began. We needed a lawyer to prepare the brief and we needed funds to pay for his services, estimated at between $5,000 and $10,000. I approached several international law firms with no success. Then I turned to individual Americans with local practices. No one had heard of the *Bellei* case, nor did they express much interest in it. To those who took the time to listen, my suggestion that an infringement of rights under citizenship law might be relevant to other rights of Americans resident overseas, perhaps even their own, fell on deaf ears. The concept was too indirect and far-reaching. I felt that this lack of response carried the implication, "You married a French man; this is the consequence," thus dismissing it as a "women's issue."

Rogge, however, took action. Writing to tell me that he had met with Eugene Girden of the Coudert Brothers law firm in New York, he said that both Girden and Alexis Coudert had a feeling for the points made in my letter and would be able to prepare an able *amicus* brief for us. I wrote to Alexis Coudert with our request that he do so.

In late October Rogge wrote that my letter had been received and that "the three of us, Coudert, Girden, and I, will have a luncheon meeting soon." Finally an answer arrived from Coudert in which he offered to write the brief. He gave a fair estimate of the costs as somewhere between $3,000 and $5,000.

It seemed astonishing that Coudert Brothers would agree to undertake such a project on behalf of an organization of 250 women with no special background or financial position. Since then I have learned that a favorable decision in the *Bellei* case would have solved several pending citizenship cases being handled by Coudert Brothers. Perhaps Charles Torem of Coudert Frères in Paris, a former president of the American Chamber of Commerce in France, had affirmed our essential reliability.

Rogge sent us a copy of his brief for the case. The argumentation was based on the Fifth Amendment to the Constitution, which guarantees due process of law. Previous decisions of the Supreme Court had confirmed the principle that Congress may not withdraw citizenship acquired by birth or by naturalization *in* the United States.

Seeking to enlarge our small group of supporters and to include American fathers, we formed an ad hoc organization called the American Dual National Citizenship Committee (ADNCC). It became the financing arm of the whole effort, which lasted until May 1971. Three people— Helen Raoul-Duval, Vivienne Fortier, and I—handled most of the administration of the campaign. Vivienne, who had served as treasurer of AAWE, agreed to carry over to the new group. As checks came in, I turned them over to her, justifiably confident that they would be properly handled. Whenever I inquired about our accounts, she could immediately tell what was in the till and what bills or expenses were pending—truly the greatest support an organization could have had.

Helen had also served her country in World War II with the State Department in Washington and then in

Algiers, Naples, Bucharest, and finally with the American Embassy in Paris. Since the death of her French husband in 1959, she had been active in the American community, notably with the American Cathedral in Paris. She had a country home to which we would retreat on weekends so I could keep up with the paperwork and she could advise me and think of people who might contribute to the cause.

We also named to the board of directors four men employed respectively by the pharmaceutical firm Squibb-Europe; the brokerage company Hayden-Stone; a management consultant firm, A. T. Kearny; and the U.S. Army. All were long-time residents of Paris, married to French citizens, and fathers of dual-national children. One, Colonel Spurgeon Boyd, had arrived in Paris with General Patton's Third Armored Tank Division. Before going on to the victory in Germany he met the young French woman who later became his wife. After twenty-five years of service around the world, he had retired in Paris and was active in both Paris Post I of the American Legion and the Benjamin Franklin Post of the Veterans of Foreign Wars.

At AAWE's well-attended November luncheon I addressed the members, presented the project, and put forth an appeal for funds. One of the women present immediately took one of the baskets used to serve bread and made her way through the room, ending up at the head table with $1,200 in pledges and checks. The members had spoken. From then on AAWE was committed to the undertaking. I was committed as well and felt both pleased and apprehensive.

As I was leaving the meeting, one of our young members eagerly informed me that her father was a lawyer and that she would write to him immediately. I encouraged her to do so, but considering the vast numbers of lawyers extant felt that nothing much would come of it. She gave no more particulars but hurried off apparently satisfied. I thought no more about her offer. We had our lawyer; the subject at hand was money.

In the middle of December everything was happening at once. Rogge wrote that the Supreme Court would hear oral arguments sometime in January. After an exchange of letters, Coudert Brothers agreed to rely on our best efforts to raise additional funds, which eased my mind considerably. A second passing of the bread basket would not be feasible until after the first of January 1970. In spite of the Christmas break in American community activities, we managed to get a request for funds mimeographed and distributed to American community organizations. The American Chamber of Commerce in France agreed to let us use its mailing address—a great help because it indicated a certain recognition of our ad hoc organization, if not actual sponsorship.

During my Christmas trip home to Washington I went to New York to meet with Coudert and Girden. In a suite of offices in the Pan American Building overlooking Park Avenue, I was received with no impression of haste, as if they had all the time we needed to discuss the matter. Coudert told me that on the very day he had received my first letter, he had seen a copy of a book titled *Another Way of Living: A Gallery of Americans Who Choose to Live in Europe*[1] on a friend's coffee table. As he picked it up, it fell open to the page that contained an interview with me carried out two years before. It was a coincidence that implied a kind of mystical thread linking events together. Heaven was on our side.

They told me that the American Bar Association (ABA) was cofiling the *amicus* brief with AAWE—the first time the ABA had ever joined another organization in such an action. The president of the ABA was a grandfather of children born overseas whose American citizenship came under the same section of the law as *Bellei*. It turned out that he was the "lawyer" father of the young AAWE member who had stopped me at our meeting in Paris. He had been able to obtain a rapid decision from the ABA, which had been absolutely necessary since the case had been put on the January docket. A draft of the brief had already been prepared by Richard N. Gardner, a law professor at Columbia University who was later named ambassador to Italy in the Carter administration.

During our meeting I described the scope of the AAWE program for children: informal English language and American history classes, play groups, summer trips to America, and even our Thanksgiving turkeys and Halloween parties. I stressed that the French Department of Education did its part in that all students begin learning English in public schools at age twelve. Back in Washington, I wrote out some of these remarks and the conclusions that might be drawn from them and sent them to New York the following day. Some of that material was incorporated into the brief. It was a very emotional moment when finally I had a copy in my hand to read. I recognized our basic premise as I had conveyed it to Rogge and Coudert: the potential value of this new generation to the United States. Our position was very clearly stated:

> The United States now maintains diplomatic relations with over one hundred foreign countries. We are members of more than seventy international organizations. We give military or economic assistance to over fifty foreign countries. Our business firms have more than $100 billion invested abroad. We need qualified people to represent our government and our private organizations in these and other relationships.

> Some of the best qualified are precisely the American children born abroad of one citizen-parent affected by section 301 (b). While retaining a strong American identity, they are usually bilingual, with a particular capacity to operate effectively in a foreign environment. They have precisely the cross-cultural facility that is essential to effective United States operations overseas. This is a facility that is hard to teach and one that our country has often found in short supply. They are a valuable national asset in an increasingly interdependent world.

Our ideas, whatever their value and whatever influence they might have, would be brought to the desks of the highest court in the land. Even now, more than two decades later, my awe at that fact and at the system of government that permits it has not diminished.

The case was heard on January 15, 1970. Both Coudert and Rogge wrote promptly, saying that the argument went well but that they would not undertake to predict the result. In what seemed to be a good sign, Justice Brennan had asked whether the law was applicable to children born to American servicemen abroad. The answer was yes. On April 29, 1970, came word from Coudert that the justices were deadlocked four to four and had decided to reargue the case during the next term, when a ninth justice would be seated. Coudert would follow through in the matter. We also heard from Rogge, who wrote, "*Bellei* will be reargued in October 1970. Deep questions take longer to decide than ordinary ones."

Approaching Congress

We sent a memorandum to everyone on our mailing list, now numbering close to 200 people, advising them of the deadlock. We also told them that Senator Edward Kennedy, (D-MA) of the Judiciary Committee and twenty-three co-sponsors had introduced a bill in December 1969 to establish a special commission whose task would be to revise the Immigration and Nationality Act. Senator Kennedy stated,

> This important segment of public policy has been ignored and overlooked by the Congress since the codification and amendment of nationality and naturalization laws in 1952. There is little doubt that many provisions in the basic statutes are products of a harsher period in our nation's history and should have no place in the public policy of a free society. The situation clearly demands a comprehensive review and evaluation of our nationality and naturalization policy. I strongly feel this will be more easily accomplished through the efforts of an independent select commission.

We told our people that it was in everyone's interest to state our case to the Senate Judiciary Committee immediately. For even if the Supreme Court decision was favorable, nothing guaranteed that Congress would not create a requirement of some other nature. On the other hand, if the Court ruled to retain the residence requirement, the next step would be to persuade Congress to repeal it by way of an amendment. We recommended that letters be written to Senator Kennedy and to the Senate Judiciary Committee and that they be sent to me for personal delivery as I would again travel to Washington for the Christmas holidays.

In Washington, I trod the hallways of congressional offices for the first time. I learned how windy it was walking from the Senate to the House side of the Hill and quickly went underground, joining the lawmakers on their special trains. I discovered the cafeteria on the ground floor of the Capitol, had my lunch, watched the people, and absorbed the atmosphere. Nothing fazed me, least of all the varied receptions offered by committee staff members: polite or indifferent, caring or uncaring. All of this was stimulating and exciting, and no matter what the conclusion, I felt that I was playing a real part in the political process. The words I said and the documents I left behind would somehow travel up the hierarchy from front office clerical staff to the members of Congress who were empowered to act.

More than thirty letters describing hardships caused by these laws were left with a staff member in Senator Kennedy's office. I left memos and press clippings on the *Bellei* case with both the Senate and the House Judiciary Committee staffs.

Included among these memos was one from Helen Raoul-Duval, a descendent of Commodore Perry, on behalf of her son. There was a letter from an attending physician at the American Hospital in Paris whose children had been born there. A retired master sergeant living in Italy wrote that he was the first American soldier to be married on the European continent after the invasion of Italy. His Italian wife had given birth to a son in October 1944. He wrote,

I was here fighting for my country when he was born. I was here with him to deter the spread of Communism when he became of the age eligible to return to the United States. You may see what a problem we had. My parents were both dead, we had no living relatives in the United States. I was able to live comfortably with the lower cost of living in Europe. I pay rather dearly to send my children to the dependent school since I have retired. I don't think my government owes me anything, but neither do I think our families should suffer because of, to my thinking, a stupid law.

Except for a few "Dear constituent" form letters, we received no written responses. We had not been put on the back burner—we had not even reached the stove.

Rogge came to Paris in May and spoke to a large audience at an AAWE luncheon. The deputy consul general was there. So was the actress Olivia de Havilland, whose daughter had been born in France of a French father.

We next mounted an effort to get coverage in American publications. Press correspondents stationed in Paris were usually willing to write a story for us, in some cases because they themselves had children born overseas. The difficulty lay in persuading the home offices that the subject would be of interest to their readers. It was easier to deal with the European English-language press. Murray Weiss, editor of the *International Herald Tribune*, was always helpful. Without the space the *Tribune* devoted to this campaign and the others that followed, I am not certain we would have been successful. The articles in the *Tribune* not only informed Americans in other countries but gave legitimacy to our efforts.

Every day brought letters. Some of the correspondents sent checks; some just told their stories. One letter from an American mother in Turkey stands out. Married to a Turkish citizen, she wrote to say that her son, who had come to the United States to fulfill the five-year residence requirement, had been drafted and sent to war in Vietnam. He had been wounded and had received a medical discharge from the service. He had been awarded six medals, including the Airman V, the Bronze Star, and the Purple

Heart, yet was informed at the American Embassy that his daughter had no rights to American citizenship. His mother wrote,

> It seems to me that something is wrong with a law which denies a young man fighting in Vietnam for his country full rights of citizenship simply because he was born abroad and was not allowed to stay five years in the country before being called upon to fight for it.

A Disappointing Outcome

The *Bellei* case was reargued on November 12, 1970. Rogge argued that once Congress had granted citizenship, it couldn't then take it away. The official transcript reads,

> I'd say on the basis of fundamental fairness this Government can't come along to someone who wants his citizenship, who had his passport for twelve years as an American citizen, and say, "Oh, by the way, we're now taking that away from you," and seek to do that without his consent.

Rogge gave half of his allotted time to Professor Gardner, who had written our brief. Justice Marshall asked Gardner whether or not these children would be willing to take an oath of allegiance to the United States at age twenty-one. Gardner answered yes. Then Marshall asked, "In what language?" Gardner replied that English would seem to be appropriate. When Marshall retorted, "What if they didn't speak English?" Gardner cited the experience of members of AAWE that the overwhelming majority of these children speak English and are brought up in an American cultural tradition. He went on to say,

> At issue today is the citizenship of the direct descendants of people who helped build America, of youngsters of value who will contribute to the future of America and of children of American citizens who have spent their productive years in the service of America. I submit that these foreign-born children are the victims of invidious discrimination. A child

of two alien parents who happens to be born in the United States during a brief visit of these parents can go back to their native land, grow up in a home in which English is not spoken, and remain an American citizen for the rest of his or her life without any residence requirements.

Also from the official record is the following exchange between a justice and Erwin N. Griswold, solicitor general of the United States:

> Mr. Solicitor General, if this Court should affirm [the constitutionality of the five-year residence requirement], do you anticipate that Congress might repeal these statutes?

> It's difficult for me, Mr. Justice, to know what Congess might do in the future. I think it is very likely that there would be a recommendation that these statutes be reworded and then be reenacted to provide that such a person becomes a citizen if he comes to the United States for five years between the ages of thirteen and twenty-eight and that in the period before he comes to the United States, he shall have *certain rights of citizenship, such as the right to enter free of quotas and to have perhaps some kind of a special document, not a passport, indicating his potential citizenship* in the United States.

In a five-to-four decision announced on April 5, 1971, the Supreme Court upheld the constitutionality of the five-year residence requirement for children born abroad of one American parent only. Justice Black, one of the dissenters, said that the ruling was evidence that the rights of Americans could fall victim to every "passing political breeze that changes the membership of the Court." The other dissenters were Justices Brennan, Douglas, and Marshall. Carl Rowan, writing in the now-defunct *Washington Star* on April 9, 1971, stated that "Congress is free to set up arbitrary standards for taking away the citizenship of those acquiring citizenship abroad, whereas it cannot strip a native-born American of citizenship. At least not yet."

We really never took the time to be disappointed at the Court's decision. By the time it was announced, we were so involved in reaching Congress that the unfavorable decision only added fuel to the flames. And as Alexis Coudert wrote to me, "We have done our best."

A Partial Victory

We now turned our full attention to Congress. Emmanuel Celler (D-NY), chairman of the House Judiciary Committee and a member of the same law firm as Rogge, lost no time in introducing a bill on May 11, 1971, proposing a reduction in the residence requirement to two years between the ages of fourteen and thirty.

Newly armed with recommendations to Congress from AAWE members, I returned to Washington in July. I was able to meet with the legal counsels of Senators Hiram Fong (R-HI) and Hugh Scott (D-PA) and with Representative Hamilton Fish, Jr. (R-NY). They and others were willing to listen and appeared to agree that the restrictions were indeed unfair.

Meanwhile Senator Kennedy had introduced yet another bill to amend the Immigration and Nationality Act, though it did not address our problem. When I found out about his bill, I went to his office again in the hope of persuading him to include our proposals. The person who received me did not know about the statement and letters from overseas Americans that I had left for the senator the previous December, nor was she disposed to look into the matter. It was a busy office. This time I was fazed and simply not able to get past her desk.

Capitol Hill was as hot in the summer as it had been cold the previous winter. Nevertheless, walking in the muggy heat from the Senate to the House side twice in one afternoon, I felt an exhilaration from the site itself—the Capitol, the House and Senate office buildings, the Supreme Court, and the Library of Congress—all on the few acres called Capitol Hill, the greatest concentration of power and learning in the world. Baking in the hot sun I somehow melted into it. It seemed to follow that if *I* belonged, so did our whole group. Eventually we would have our way.

I wondered what my great-grandfather would have thought of my mission. After serving in the Michigan Cavalry during the Civil War, he had come to Washington and became a dealer in building materials, furnishing Vermont granite for the Capitol building itself. My grandmother had been raised four blocks away and had lived nearby after her marriage.

After my setback in the senator's office, I started in on the telephone, beginning with the State Department. My primary question was who counts lengths of residence for citizenship purposes, whether it is the ten years required of the American-citizen parent (with foreign spouse) to transmit to a child born overseas, or the five years the child needs to maintain the citizenship? I also had several secondary questions: How is residence officially established? If someone comes to the United States to fulfill the requirement, is there some kind of declaration of arrival to be filed with the State Department or with the INS? Is there an administrative procedure for determining arrivals and departures during the residence period? Who checks? Is there an office in Washington or in embassies overseas where a declaration might be made at the beginning or end of the five-year period? What documents constitute proof of residence—school records, affadivits, entry and exit stamps in passports?

The State Department's answers were specific and vague at the same time. There was no set list of documents to have available to back up one's claims, but having certain records would help establish proof of residence.

Then I tried the INS, asking the same questions and receiving basically the same answers. There was no specific administrative procedure and no formal declaration to make upon beginning or ending the residence periods. Passed from one person to another, I rose ever higher in the organization, eventually reaching General Counsel Charles Gordon, who invited me to come and see him the following day.

He received me flanked by three subordinates. There I was, facing four empowered officials. They were not necessarily hostile but were obviously in authority. Gordon said magnanimously, "Now, I wouldn't want you to think your government does not want to listen to you." Another, more sharply, asked, "Why don't these women come home to have their babies?" I described the difficulties of traveling, the expense, and the concerns about care for siblings during the mother's absence. I told them about husbands wishing to be present for the birth but prevented by their professional responsibilities. If the expectant mother had no family or friends to receive her, she would be alone. She would have to pay the costs not only of the hospital but also of the stay in a hotel before and after the birth. Granting citizenship under these conditions would amount to making it available to some but not to others— not a very democratic way of doing things.

Attempting to present a complete picture, I spoke of the potential value of this new European-American generation even as future employees of the federal government. There are positions where the ability to understand and negotiate in a foreign culture is absolutely necessary. Why push these dual national Americans away, effectively handing them over to the country of the foreign parent?

I was then asked more questions in a softer tone. What did my husband do for a living? Why didn't he immigrate to America? I answered that he managed a profitable family business working, in fact, with American exporters. He was a responsible man, a good father with a wife and two children to support. Leaving France would mean exchanging a satisfactory situation for a precarious one. He was content to be French and felt no need to become an American citizen. They seemed somewhat surprised at that, so I added a question of my own: Did they really want reluctant immigrants? My husband had no objection to the American citizenship of our children, and as French law accepted double nationality, there was no problem as far as he was concerned.

Gordon told me that initial hearings on the Celler bill, which reduced the five-year residence requirement to two years, had already been held in Texas on provisions dealing with Mexican immigrants and that someone from AAWE should attend the next set of hearings, which would be held in Washington early in 1972. There was a cordial ending to the meeting. I felt that they had truly listened and gained some understanding of our position. It was obvious, though, that the large numbers of Mexican immigrants would bear more heavily on their final opinion.

I then called upon Arlene Tuck Ulman, the Washington representative of the American Bar Association, to get a copy of our *amicus* brief. I wanted to give it to an assistant of Senator Fong, whom I had seen the previous week. It turned out that Ulman and the assistant, a Mrs. Parker, had been in the same class at law school, as had Alexis Coudert. When I told her I had just left the general counsel, she burst into smiles. She knew "Charlie" and his wife well—they played bridge every Friday night! In citizenship matters it was a small world at the top.

Ulman strongly recommended that members of the AAWE be present for the Washington hearings. As Ulman was fully aware of our situation and our previous actions, it appeared expedient to ask her to represent us. She agreed to appear at the hearings and to do it for a very modest fee. Back in Paris I reported to the AAWE board, which approved the action.

We began yet another letter-writing campaign, this time to Peter Rodino (D-NJ), chairman of the House Judiciary Committee. We sought out cases in which there was no second nationality for the individuals to fall back on. In these cases noncompliance would leave the person stateless. We gathered another batch of letters setting forth the family hardships caused by the law and sent them to Ulman to be presented at the hearings.

Several letters were from people who had served in the U.S. Army. The daughter of one of them had been born in a U.S. military hospital in Germany and had resided in the United States for more than ten years during her father's Stateside military assignments. But they were the wrong years. The law required five years' residence after the age of fourteen. She had passed her twenty-third birthday and could not meet the requirement. Her father wrote,

This is not my fault, nor hers, inasmuch as foreign service assignments for military personnel are not of individual choice. We of the military have more than our share of hardships, hazardous duty assignments, family separations, and financial problems incident thereto; but to add this further degrading hardship concerning the citizenship of a child just because of its place of birth is unjust, unmoral, and without reason.

Another retired veteran, disabled from wounds received in the Battle of the Bulge, wrote that some of his ancestors had fought in the War of Independence, his grandfathers in the Civil War, and his father in the Spanish-American War. He wrote:

We hope that our fifteen-year-old son will be able to continue his education in the United States, but for financial reasons it is most unlikely he will be able to fulfill the residence requirement by his twenty-eighth birthday.

There was a letter from a former Fulbright scholar, who wrote that she had met her husband, also a Fulbright scholar, at the University of Indiana. She was one of six American teachers who in 1972 constituted the American Section in the International Lycée (high school) in St. Germain-en-Laye helping 150 American students adjust to their French curriculum while keeping up with American studies at the level they would have at home. She wrote,

Besides our teaching duties we act as public relations agents for America: giving concerts, producing plays, participating in international seminars, etc. Last spring fifty French high school supervisors enthusiastically applauded our simulated classroom demonstrations of American teaching methods. They were amazed at the student-teacher rapport. The American Section also had the honor of working with the committee, which first devised the International Baccalaureat Exam, the first to provide an equitable evaluation of students' high school work in various countries. Throughout the world there are Americans like myself who spend their lives pro-moting American language and culture. Their children are born abroad and grow up perfectly bilingual, rich with a dual culture. Then, just when they are ripe to return to America bearing the wealth of two or more languages and an intimate understanding of the European mentality, when they represent a potential gold mine for American commerce, international relations, or education, they lose their American citizenship for not having resided in the States when their parents felt them too young to live away from them for so many years.

Another letter emphasizing the perils of statelessness came from an American engineer working in Morocco on projects financed by the Agency for International Development. His two daughters were born in Morocco, but under Moroccan law they could not claim citizenship by reason of birth. Under the law of Portugal their mother, a Portuguese citizen, could not transmit her citizenship. If they were unable to complete the required residence in the United States, they would be left with no citizenship and would become stateless.

Ulman attended the hearings and spoke for all of us with great success. The new law (P.L. 92-584), dated October 27, 1972, reduced the residence period from five years to two, to be accomplished between the ages of fourteen and twenty-eight.

Three years had passed since November 1969, when AAWE joined the action in *Bellei* v. *Rogers*. But this time we had won!

Notes

1.   John Bainbridge, *Another Way of Living: A Gallery of Americans Who Choose to Live in Europe* (New York: Holt, Rinehart & Winston, 1968).

4

A Successful Campaign (1973–1975)

From TIME to time I looked for a job as my children were growing up. I read and spoke French with ease, but I had never mastered French verb endings. I could spell in my own language, however, so I always began my search with the personnel office of the American Embassy. Their practice of not employing American citizens resident in France remained in effect. It was especially galling to encounter that policy in the consular section. Since a consulate must deal with U.S. citizens, their passports, registration of births, information on Social Security benefits, plus the many problems tourists encounter, it just didn't make sense. Citizens of other countries—the French, the British, or the Irish—were employed in these local-hire positions. Apparently anyone was eligible except U.S. citizens. I heartily resented this State Department policy.

Perseverance pays, however, and in the spring of 1973 I joined the staff of the American Chamber of Commerce in France. Founded in 1894 by a group of American and French businessmen, it was the first chamber of commerce established outside the United States. Some of the original members were American Express, Singer Sewing Machine, and the *New York Herald Tribune*. Office space was donated by Coudert Frères, one of the first international law firms. After World War I, such well-known companies as Carnation Milk, Palmolive, Otis Elevator, Westinghouse, General Electric, United Shoe Machinery, Western Electric, Eastman Kodak, and International Harvester became members of the Chamber.[1]

While working at the Chamber I learned of other inequities in American laws that affect the personnel of international firms. One of these was Medicare. American citizens traveling or residing overseas had been excluded from the original Medicare law. Medical expenses incurred outside of the United States are not covered, the rationale being that it is not possible to control the quality of care given by institutions and medical personnel in foreign countries. However, many private insurance companies were and still are able to deal with foreign hospitals. The federal government could do the same.

Thérèse Bonney, an American journalist, correspondent, and photographer in both world wars, instigated one of the first efforts to correct the situation. She formed the Paris Medicare Committee, which drafted and circulated a petition addressed to the Secretary of Health, Education and Welfare (HEW). Her petition was signed by nineteen American nonprofit organizations in France. There was no response of any consequence from HEW.

Another fundamental problem for Americans overseas was that of absentee voting. An estimated 750,000 overseas voters were effectively disenfranchised because it was so difficult to obtain an absentee ballot from their home state. Archaic procedural requirements posed significant barriers. About half of the states made no provision for absentee registration. Louisiana, for example, would only allow absentee balloting for students, military personnel, and other employees of the U.S. government. Home states varied, but complaints from disgruntled voters were similar: "Ohio does not register foreign residents, even now"; "We fought a war concerning taxation without representation"; and "I have not voted since joining the foreign service in 1945 because I was abroad or in Washington and could not be in New Jersey at the time needed for personally registering." Many lamented that because county clerk offices did not use airmail postage, their ballot arrived when the election was over. Some states would tax former residents even if they did not own property in that state.

As for citizenship laws, although the amendment of 1972 had reduced the residence requirement for children born overseas of one American parent, there were other snags. An American parent married to a foreign national could not transmit citizenship to a child born overseas without having resided ten years in the U.S. prior to the birth of the child.

There was also the risk of loss of citizenship for certain acts, one of which was becoming a citizen of a foreign country. We had received a letter from an American woman married to a English diplomat. British law required that she become a British citizen. But if she did, American law would bar her U.S. citizenship. If she did not become a British citizen, her husband would be obliged to resign from the British foreign office and face the loss of a promising career. British law seemed to be more liberal than American law, for it had no objection to her retaining her U.S. citizenship when and if she became a British national.

There was the same risk of losing American citizenship for those who had acquired a second nationality under conditions acceptable to the law. Many were teaching American history or English in French public schools. According to one section of the Immigration and Nationality Act, this constituted "working for a foreign government," for which the same penalty could be exacted. It was especially nonsensical to chastise individuals who were disseminating American language and culture. For the most part this difficulty was avoided by working on a temporary contract basis, but in such a case the American teacher forfeited certain job-related benefits, such as tenure.

The Association of American Residents Overseas

In the spring of 1973 Jean Archbold, Sonja Mincbere, and Helen Raoul-Duval returned to Paris from a Federation of Women's Clubs Overseas (FAWCO) conference convinced that the time had come to create a new organization. It would focus on all of the issues just described but would also address what ~~what~~ we were beginning to see as the underlying cause: the generally unfavorable image of American citizens overseas. I met with them, and we agreed that the key to success would be ending the problems associated with absentee voting. Votes were the best way to influence Congress to consider the problems of overseas Americans.

We concluded that a task of equal consequence was to bring together the disparate groups within American overseas communities. The businessmen, their families, federal government personnel, those employed by ~~private~~ private voluntary organizations, and the self-employed could be made to see that they were all connected, at least insofar as their citizenship rights were concerned. Thus, an advance upon the Medicare front, even though of special concern to retirees, would have a positive even if indirect effect on citizenship matters of more interest to younger people. The object would be to have the individuals who made up these groups act in unison, putting forth efforts and approaches to Congress on all issues alike.

We decided that the new organization should be headed by a man so that it would not be perceived as being limited to "women's issues." Our original committee of four chose Randolph A. Kidder, a retired foreign service officer who had served as ambassador to Cambodia and was associated with The Conference Board, a business research group, in Paris. His background combining both business experience and diplomatic service was just what was needed.

Over a pleasant lunch on the Boulevard St. Germain, we persuaded him with no great difficulty to lend his talents to the cause. He served as president for four years. Generally affable in all circumstances, he would fold notices and stuff envelopes with the rest of us during board meetings. When we held conferences, he introduced guests and steered us through the agenda with easy eloquence.

Soon thereafter, meeting in the home of Helen Raoul-Duval, we took the first steps. Each of us contributed $100 to constitute an operating fund. Sonja agreed to the use of her home address for mailing purposes. It didn't take much more; we were in business. We chose as our name the Association of American Residents Overseas (AARO). I agreed to act as executive secretary and remained in that position for four years.

Our next recruit was Vivienne Fortier, who had served as treasurer of AAWE during its fledgling years and had assumed the same duties when we financed the Supreme Court brief in the *Bellei* case. It just seemed right and natural to be able to count on her.

To get us off to a good start, we sought a public announcement of some kind. This we did by way of a letter to the editor in the *International Herald Tribune*. Published on July 24, 1973, it read in part,

A third of the two and one-half million Americans living and working outside of the United States are taxed without being represented in Congress. They are the 750,000 Americans effectively disenfranchised by archaic state voting regulations. Those who, having no representation in Congress, are practically powerless to influence the enactment of legislation which may affect them adversely.

Americans resident, say, in Belgium, Australia, or Brazil cannot be consulted upon proposed changes in laws which concern them nor can they initiate action for amendments in citizenship laws, tax laws, and regulations of various government administrations, simply because no official and specific channels exist through which they may state their views. Most of them probably do not even know when legislation pertinent to their civil rights is under way, for there has been

no one organization to speak for all of them, to speak to
them and through which they may communicate.

Will Congress finally act in the light of the obvious fact that
Americans living and working outside of the United States
are not "expatriates" nor are they second-class citizens who
can be deprived of such normal rights as Medicare? They
constitute a large task force of first-class citizens who maintain their country's commercial, political, cultural, industrial,
and technical position throughout the world. They deserve
to be respected, not rebuffed.

The publication of that letter was quickly followed
by a lively correspondence in the editorial section, beginning with a retort by Sid Berstein, a retired naval officer,
who wrote that he would take away all citizenship rights
of any American who had worked overseas for over one
year. Of the many answers to Berstein published throughout July and August, one said that the essential issue is the
constitutional right of all American citizens, wherever they
may be, to vote in U.S. national elections.

The Bipartisan Committee on Absentee Voting

AARO was not the first organization to represent Americans abroad with the goal of correcting inequities across
the board, but it has been among the most successful.[2] One
of its first actions was to associate itself with the Bipartisan
Committee on Absentee Voting, which had been established in Paris in 1969 by Alfred E. Davidson, an international lawyer. Davidson's career in government service
following World War II had begun with the United Nations Refugee and Reconstruction Agency (UNRRA). Sub-
sequently he had organized the conduct of relief supplies
to the Middle East and Africa, become a director of the
United Nations International Children's Emergency Fund
(UNICEF) in Paris, and been a member of the personal

staff of Trygvie Lie, then secretary general of the United Nations, before joining the World Bank. As a Democrat, he later coordinated the presidential campaigns of George McGovern and Jimmy Carter in France. A second founder of the Bipartisan Committee was Richard H. Moore, a lawyer with Cleary, Gottlieb, Steen & Hamilton in Paris, who at that time was serving as president of the American Chamber of Commerce in France. On the Republican side were Harvey Gerry, a banker; Clement Brown, an executive with Olin Corporation who had first come to France in 1944 by way of Omaha Beach; and David McGovern, an international lawyer who had resided in Paris since 1967. An associated Businessmen's Committee was composed of executives with such firms as Pan American, American Express, Ferguson Morrison Knudson, Philip Morris, Ashland Oil and Refining, and IBM Europe. Pierre Salinger and Clement Brown served as its honorary chairmen.

A letter from the Bipartisan Committee to American firms in France that was undated but mailed sometime before July 30, 1969, sought "reasonable contributions" to cover the $6000 cost of an *amicus curiae* brief in a Supreme Court case to review state absentee-voting requirements. The letter pointed out that "the case in question, *Halls* v. *Beals*, could be the wedge by which unreasonable state residence requirements are declared unconstitutional and could help our American employees obtain their voting rights." The brief quoted Attorney General John N. Mitchell:

A residency requirement for local elections is to insure that the new resident has sufficient time to familiarize himself with local issues. But such requirements have no relevance to presidential elections because the issues tend to be nationwide in scope and receive nationwide dissemination by the communications media. The President is the representative of all the people and all the people should have a reasonable opportunity to vote for him.

In July 1973 the Bipartisan Committee opened an office in Washington under the leadership of J. Kevin Murphy, who was then president of Purolator Services and later president of the Chamber of Commerce of the United States. Eugene Marans of the Washington office of Cleary, Gottlieb, Steen & Hamilton took the lead in the campaign for the passage of the Overseas Citizens Absentee Voting Rights Act of 1975. For over two years, Marans never let up in his *pro bono* effort to get a voting rights bill through Congress and on the president's desk for his signature.

On June 25, 1973, Senator Charles McC. Mathias, Jr. (R-MD), introduced a bill to abolish domicile and residence requirements as preconditions for absentee voting in federal elections. The bill called for a federal registration procedure in which a postcard form would be accepted by the states as an application for an absentee ballot. It was referred to the Privileges and Elections Subcommittee of the Senate Rules and Administration Committee. Soon afterward, Senator Claiborne Pell (D-RI) introduced a similar bill. As the Mathias bill began wending its way through the legislative process, hearings were held in the Senate on September 26 and 27, 1973. Several former U.S. ambassadors testified on behalf of the legislation, among them Sargent Shriver, Charles E. Bohlen, Chester Bowles, Averill Harriman, Arthur Goldberg, and George Bush. The Justice Department, wary of potential voter fraud, came out against the bill. A deputy assistant attorney general stated that

> it seems basically unfair to permit a person residing abroad, who may have no knowledge of or interest in the state or district in which he was formerly domiciled, to cast votes in that state or district.

After the hearings the bill was assigned to the Elections Subcommittee of the House Administration Committee, which was chaired by John Dent (D-PA).

Once legislation had been introduced in both the House and the Senate, the next step was to get it moving. The path went from the subcommittee to the full committee, to hearings, then back to the committee, which would integrate the recommendations of the federal agencies that would administer the law. It would then go to the floor of each house for a vote. Once past that hurdle, it went to the White House. All of this had to be accomplished before the end of the year because bills that are not passed must be reintroduced in the next session of Congress, whereupon the whole process starts over again.

Letters from overseas Americans were needed at every step; they were the best way to influence members of Congress. We put together a mailing list by contacting American social groups, men's and women's clubs, university alumni associations, veterans' groups, press correspondents, churches, and schools, and Democratic and Republican committees anywhere in the world where we could stir up a contact. Our goal was to inform as many individuals as possible that the bill had been introduced and what it would accomplish, and then encourage them to write, phone, or cable members of Congress to urge passage of the bill. The bill's name and number, a sample letter, and the name and address of their member of Congress were needed.

At the same time, we set up a system for communicating with groups and individuals on our list. Word of action on the bills in both houses of Congress would arrive by telex from Marans in the Cleary, Gottlieb, Steen & Hamilton office in Washington to their Paris office. They would call me at the chamber of commerce and read the message. I would then compose and type up a news flash, have it mimeographed, then fold it into a set of preaddressed envelopes. Within a couple of hours, the word would go out to our key people throughout Europe. In the days before the Internet, this was considered rapid action.

Not all of the individuals in one particular region were able or disposed to move quickly. But there was usually one person in each country who accorded the news flash top priority. For example, the long-time executive director of the American Chamber of Commerce in Italy, Herman H. Burdick, was assiduous in disseminating what we sent to him. The now-defunct *Rome Daily American* always covered events and devoted ample space to the initiatives taken in Washington and elsewhere.[3] We had similar contacts in Amsterdam, London, Brussels, Frankfurt, and other cities. I did not know them all, nor can I now remember every individual with whom we corresponded. But one certainty remains: those American citizens wanted to vote.

Our news flashes were backed up by short ads in the *International Herald Tribune*. Davidson authored most of them, with titles like "More Letters to Mathias," "Focus on Frenzel," "Deluge Dent," "This Is Wiggens Week," "Calling All Californians," "Wiggens is Wavering," "Go after Gaydoes," "Voting Bill Moves Ahead," and "Your Letters Are Working!"

The Justice Department continued to oppose the legislation upon the grounds that voter fraud would occur. It was willing, however, to withdraw all objections except insofar as voting rights would be extended to persons "who have established a foreign domicile." Our news flash of May 9, 1974, urged overseas Americans to write to Senator Mathias stating that Americans overseas were required by the host country to establish domiciliation and that this had nothing to do with their right to vote. Furthermore, if the law excluded those who had established a foreign domicile, it would exclude practically everyone for whom the bill was originally intended.

The Absentee Voting Rights Act

The bill did not pass in 1974. But on the second day after the opening of the Ninety-fourth Congress, Senator Mathias reintroduced it as S.-95, the Overseas Citizens Absentee Voting Rights Act. Cosponsors included Senators Claiborne Pell (D-RI), Barry Goldwater (R-AZ), Birch Bayh (D-IN), William Brock (R-TN), and William V. Roth (R-DE). The House version of the bill was introduced on February 19, 1975, by Representatives John Dent (D-PA) and Wayne Hays (D-OH). Similar bills were presented by Representatives

Bill Frenzel (R-MN) and Gilbert Gude (R-MD). The House Elections Subcommittee held hearings in February and March. Senator Goldwater told the Senate that he believed the right to vote was an inherent part of U.S. citizenship and not a prerogative right of the states. Sargent Shriver complained that "Americans abroad not only lack the opportunity to participate, they are excluded from representation."

Good fortune for this legislation came to us in the form of Sonja Beaumont Mincbere. A linguist, Sonja was brought up speaking Russian, English, and French. During her studies abroad she also learned German and Polish. In World War II she saw duty in the European theater as a captain with the U.S. Army. After the war she served as liaison officer with the war crimes branch in Wiesbaden and as an observer in Nuremberg. In 1947 she set up the French and Polish courses at the Army language school in Monterey, California. She met her French husband in 1949 while serving as a foreign service officer at the American Embassy in Paris. That exceptional background, together with her experience as president of both AAWE and FAWCO, certainly overqualified her for the job of vice president of AARO. But Sonja, knowledgeable, sophisticated, and elegant, was never superficial. She took on the job of keeping our mailing list up to date and posting dues payments and address changes on five-by-eight index cards in the library of the Chamber of Commerce, where I had my desk. She sat at one of the big tables surrounded by reference volumes and other business publications.

When the day began to seem long, Sonja and I would take a break and walk down a long hallway into the kitchen to have a cup of tea. One day we discussed the difficulties of generating letters to members of Congress and arousing their interest to act upon those that they did receive. The latter problem was rendered even more difficult by the fact that the people writing the letters were not actual but only potential constituents. Good as it was, our system of eliciting letters—explaining what to say and when—was unwieldy. We needed something simple, direct, and catchy.

Suddenly Sonja picked up a tea bag, took a good look at it, waved it around, and said, "Tea Party, Boston." She had found our gimmick.

We wrote a letter to be sent to members of Congress and typed it out on a sheet of AARO letterhead:

> In 1773, there was a Tea Party because of no representation. In 1975, we mail you this tea bag because of the Overseas Citizens' Voting Rights Act. So that in 1976, we will be able to vote for you. Support H.R.-3211 and S.-95.

We drew up a short cover letter, asking the recipient to staple a tea bag to the enclosed letter and mail it to their representatives in Congress. The mailing addresses of the House and Senate were added. All we had to do then was to send one copy to our working people in other cities so that they could make multiple copies and send it to the people on their mailing list. It was a clever idea, and it worked.

On December 10, 1975, a telex arrived from Marans informing us that the reconciliation bill had passed the House that afternoon, 374 to 43. He commented that the bill's opponents "realized [their] number was up when minority leader John Rhodes (R-AZ) made a five-minute speech urging adoption of the bill." Wayne L. Hays (D-OH), chairman of the House Administration Committee, made a big point about the amount of mail favoring the bill that had been received in his office—it exceeded by five or six times the amount that had come in on any other issue before his committee that year. The tea bag campaign had won the day.

But although we had prevailed in Congress, we were threatened by defeat in the White House. Opposition by the Justice Department continued, led by Antonin Scalia, who was then the legal counsel to the Assistant Attorney General and later appointed to the Supreme Court by President Ronald Reagan. He disagreed with the constitutionality of the law and pursuaded the attorney general to continue to oppose the president's signature. The bill had to be signed by the end of the congressional session or it was doomed to return once again to the starting point. Marans, seeing the end of the year rapidly approaching, decided to go over the head of the Justice Department. He asked Senator Barry Goldwater to call the legal counsel of President Ford. Senator Goldwater's message to the White House was:

Listen, you damned fools, there are more Republicans in Paris than there are in Detroit, and Ford doesn't want to be the first president to veto a voting rights bill since the Reconstruction.

The bill was signed by the president on January 2, 1976. It was the first legislation on voting passed by Congress since Reconstruction that has never been subject to a constitutional challenge. Americans can now register and vote absentee in the presidential and congressional primaries and elections from the state in which they last resided.

Without the constant efforts of Eugene Marans, who persuaded members of Congress, talked to Justice Department officials, and prepared presentations for congressional hearings, it is clear that the bill would never have passed or have been signed by the president.

Our final ad in the *Tribune* suggested one more set of letters to members of Congress to thank them for the passage of the law. We recomended that the letter be signed by the writer as a new constituent. We extended our special gratitude for the constant support of Senators Goldwater, Pell, and Mathias, and Representatives Frenzel, Hays, Dent, and Rhodes.

Direct political life had begun for the 3 million Americans resident overseas. In every election since 1976, American organizations overseas, including the committees of both the Democratic and Republican parties, have expanded their information programs and voter rallies at election times. In 1993 the international edition of *USA Today,* citing Phyllis Taylor, director of the Federal Voter Assistance Program, reported that absentee ballots may have turned the tide in elections in California, Georgia, Maryland, Minnesota, Nevada, New York, North Dakota, South Dakota, Texas, and Washington.

Notes

1. The American Chamber of Commerce in Paris is autonomous but is part of a European network that constitutes the European Council of American Chambers of Commerce (ECACC). The newest members come from Eastern Europe: Warsaw, Bucharest, Bratislava, and Prague. They are linked by regional councils in Europe, Asia, and South America. The ECACC works together with the commercial and economic sections of American embassies. It also acts in concert with the Council of American States in Europe, which is made up of thirty-seven offices in Europe representing thirty-two states of the Union. Their objective is to encourage European investments in their states and to increase exports of their agricultural and manufactured products. Seven port authorities from the states of California, Delaware, Illinois, Maryland, New Jersey, New York, Oregon, and Virginia also maintain offices in Europe.

2. Organizations of Americans resident overseas, both past and present, are described in Appendix A.

3. The *Rome Daily American* began publication in 1945 as an outgrowth of the wartime edition of the *Stars and Stripes;* it was published until 1975. At its peak 16,000 copies a day were distributed throughout the Mediterranean region.

5

Temporary Setbacks (1976–1977)

IN THE mid-1970s, informal Democratic Party groups were organized into official committees in Europe, Israel, and Canada. Carl Ross, a pioneer advocate of the rights of overseas citizens, set up a committee in Mexico City. The groups were linked together and to Democratic Party headquarters in Washington by an administrative structure first called the Democratic Party Committee Abroad (DPCA) and now known simply as Democrats Abroad. Anthony (Toby) Hyde, a former member of Truman's White House staff who lived in London, succeeded Alfred Davidson as head of Democrats Abroad in 1976. It was he who persuaded the Democratic National Committee to recognize delegates to represent overseas citizens at the Democratic National Convention. The first election of overseas delegates took place in June 1976. Six delegates and three alternates were elected from among thirty-nine candidates residing in eleven countries. By 1992 there were twenty-two delegates plus two alternates to the National Convention in New York. The delegates control nine votes.

Republicans Abroad developed with similar speed but with a different administrative structure. The chairs of its country committees are linked directly to the chair of Republicans Abroad at the Republican National Committee's headquarters in Washington. They are an official auxiliary of the Republican National Committee and are allowed representation on the executive committee, but no delegates are allocated to participate in the National Convention. Since 1976 both Democrats and Republicans Abroad have campaigned among overseas voters for the presidential elections.

Contacts with the Democratic National Committee headquarters in Washington were less than ideal. As overseas Americans had never voted in large numbers, there was greater recognition of state delegations. It took a while for headquarters to notice the existence of this new bloc of voters.

Later that year, at a meeting of the heads of Democratic Party committees in Europe, Gerald Rafshoon, media manager for Jimmy Carter, made a pitch for our help in registering overseas voters and convincing them to vote Democratic. We suggested that Carter appeal directly to the American voter overseas. Such an appeal might take the form of a mention in a campaign speech or, better still, a letter to the overseas committees that could be widely distributed. Since that time, headquarters of both political parties seem to have recognized the large numbers of Americans residing abroad. In 1990, greetings from both candidates were addressed to overseas voters. A letter from George Bush stated that "As unofficial Ambassadors of the United States, you have helped to foster respect around the world for democratic ideals and free market principles."

By 1992, things were even better. Bill Clinton addressed a problem of overseas residents with a pledge to simplify absentee voting rules and promised "that officials of my administration will be specifically designated to study your needs and hear your comments."

These remarks were widely distributed through newsletters to members of the overseas party committees, Republican and Democratic alike. They were also published in the international edition of *USA Today* on September 26, 1992. To what extent these remarks originate with the overseas party committees, to be dispatched to Washington and bounced back to the senders as rhetoric, is anybody's guess.

Before proposing changes in laws or procedures, members of Congress want to know how many people will be affected by new legislation, in what manner, and above all what the costs will be. In effect, what would make a *real* difference in getting Congress and the White House to develop a more positive attitude toward overseas Americans would be an effort to gather substantial data about overseas citizens.

It is not known how many Americans reside abroad permanently. What are their ages, their level of education, their income? What states do they come from? What countries are they living in and how long is the average length of stay overseas? How many retirees are living on the American continent or in Europe? What are they doing overseas? What percentage of them are employed by government, in business, or with private voluntary organizations? How much do they contribute to the U.S. economy in repatriated profits and personal income tax revenues? An AARO survey conducted in 1974 sought to provide a basic profile of American families living in France. The 1,545 respondents represented 6 percent of the estimated 25,000 Americans living there at the time. The findings were analyzed by Hudson-Europe, an independent research institute then under the direction of William Pfaff. It was published in the official organ of the American Chamber of Commerce in France in January 1975.

There were a total of 1,044 family units, of which 54 percent lived in Paris and another 26 percent in the suburbs of Paris. Some 77 percent were married and 60 percent had children. Of the total of 1,176 children, some 217 were over the age of eighteen. About one-third of the Americans had come from New York State and about 14 percent from California, followed by Illinois with 6 percent and Massachusetts with 4 percent. Other states with significant representation overseas were New Jersey,

Connecticut, Pennsylvania, Michigan, and Ohio. The remaining families came from Virginia, Texas, the District of Columbia, Florida, and Minnesota. To round out the report, the Hudson Institute added a statistic from its own sources:

> Seven percent of the total profits of American business in 1974 was repatriated profit from the foreign operations of American business. American businessmen abroad had contributed to making that 7 percent of all corporate and business profits, yet their number was far below 1 percent of the American population.

But the new law that facilitated absentee voting and called for surveys of overseas citizens had no affect on the problems caused by citizenship laws. Once again the attention of the citizenship committees of AAWE and AARO was drawn to the difficulties of American women married to foreign citizens. Those who were obliged to acquire the citizenship of their country of residence faced the risk of loss of U.S. citizenship under section 349 (a) (1).[1]

Caught Between Two Countries

I had received a letter, obviously written in state of distress, from an American woman living in Hamburg, Germany. Her name was Becky Tan. American born, in her early twenties she had gone to Germany to study. There she had met and married a man of Chinese descent who had been born in Indonesia. Because of laws in effect in Indonesia at the time of his birth, he was stateless but had managed to become a resident of Germany, where he had earned a degree in medicine. After fourteen years of residence he had applied for German citizenship. Under German law his wife and children were obliged to be naturalized at the same time, but before taking this step Tan had visited the American consulate and conferred with the vice consul. He told her that she would have to take her chances on keeping or losing her American citizenship. In accordance with the law her case could not be determined until she actually took the step of becoming a German citizen. At that time a memorandum would be submitted to the State Department outlining all of the facts of the particular situation and a decision would be made by the State Department legal office. Tan, acting under the pressure of obtaining German nationality for her husband but with no intention of giving up her U.S. citizenship, made application for German citizenship for herself and their children in August 1971. As part of the German administrative paperwork, she was asked to surrender her U.S. passport. She fully expected it to be returned. However, German officials sent it to the American consulate with a statement that she was now a German citizen!

At the request of the vice consul, Tan wrote out a statement asserting that she had acquired German citizenship under duress and that she had never intented to abandon her American nationality. The statement and her passport were sent to Washington for a decision. For several months she was in limbo, waiting for the State Department to make a decision. But facing an urgent need to travel outside of Germany, she applied for and received German passports for herself and her children.

At last, five months later, a favorable decision came from Washington and her passport and those of her children were returned. Whenever she traveled to the United States she used her American passport to enter, but in order to reenter Germany she had to use her German passport. There was no other way. As the Germans considered her a German citizen, she could not be issued either a visa or a residence permit, documents that pertained to foreigners. As both the German and American governments had issued her passports, she considered herself a legal and aboveboard dual national, a citizen of two countries.

Five years later she returned to the American consulate in order to renew her passport. She was received by a German employee who asked whether she had a German passport and if it had been used. She answered yes. The employee then told her that she could not be issued a new passport because she had violated U.S. law. Furthermore, she was required to submit an affidavit, to be sent to Washington, which the employee then proceeded to dictate! When Tan refused to write out the affadavit, the employee finally called in the American consul. Tan, believing that the problem would be settled quickly, asked that he refer to her file. But the consular officer told her that she should not have a German passport and that her case had to be resubmitted to Washington.

It was at this point that she wrote to me. By then AAWE's citizenship committee had accumulated some experience with citizenship problems and felt competent to give advice. We recommended that she fight the consulate's decision. This she did, at a high cost in both financial and emotional terms.

Five months later Tan's U.S. citizenship and that of her children were reaffirmed by the State Department. State Department officials had decided that Becky Tan had acquired German citizenship under duress. Her action had not been voluntary. Their decision was communicated by cable to the consulate, which then informed Tan. She encountered no further difficulties.[2]

Addressing Medicare

While AAWE was attending to citizenship laws, overseas Democratic Party committees began to focus on the Medicare problem. They were able to have a resolution inserted into the 1976 party platform: "We believe that Medicare should be made available to Americans abroad who are eligible for Social Security."

Alfred Davidson lost no time in activating the Bipartisan Committee for Medicare Overseas. But the committee's campaign began on a disappointing note: Wilbur Cohen, a former Secretary of Health, Education and

Welfare who had worked on setting up the original Medicare bill, revealed that the question of entitlement for overseas residents and for U.S. residents traveling abroad had never been posed. Coverage of these two categories of citizens had been omitted because of concern about administrative problems it would entail, and he therefore did not support our position. (Cohen later changed his mind and became a witness for a Medicare bill at hearings in 1978.)

In September 1976 Davidson was instrumental in the introduction of a bill to extend Medicare benefits to Americans living or traveling overseas. It provided for agreements between the United States and foreign countries for payment of expenses incurred in any hospital that was accredited by the Joint Commission on the Accreditation of Hospitals or any other hospitals that met recognized health and safety standards. Under such an agreement, a person eligible for Medicare in the United States would receive the same level of care in a foreign country in which he or she resided or was traveling. Similarly, a citizen of that nation living or traveling in the United States would be eligible for government-paid health care at the level of his or her entitlement at home. At that time an estimated 189,000 people would have been eligible for coverage under such agreements. Of that number, nearly one-third lived in Canada and Mexico, with an estimated 30,000 in Italy, 12,000 in West Germany, 10,000 in England, and about 3,000 in France.

The Bipartisan Committee had obtained the backing of American organizations around the world, including the American Chambers of Commerce in Europe, Thailand, Argentina, Colombia, and Mexico, and American clubs in Europe, Spain, Portugal, Germany, Switzerland, and England.

Home for Christmas in 1976, I met with Davidson, who was also in Washington visiting his family. Together we called upon William Yoffee, HEW's international liaison officer and Paul Rettig, counsel to the Health Subcommittee of the House Ways and Means Committee. We were hopeful that the bill, which had received no attention in

1976, would be reintroduced in 1977 and that we could look forward to hearings in the spring. Robert Cutler, acting chairman of the Republican National Committee, and Robert Strauss, chairman of the Democratic National Committee, were the honorary chairmen of the Bipartisan Committee; thus, the bill was assured of bipartisan sponsorship. When Davidson conferred with Strauss he took me with him. I was very impressed and understood in my very minor role what the draw of power in Washington must be.

That summer, Davidson held other meetings on the Medicare legislation. He talked again with HEW officials and with Representative Dan Rostenkowski (D-IL), chairman of the House Ways and Means Committee. He also conferred with representatives of the American Association of Retired Persons (AARP), who agreed to back the legislation, and with directors of the International Division of the Chamber of Commerce of the United States.

In September 1978, the House approved the bill by a very favorable margin, 398 to 2. Rostenkowski's sponsorship tipped the scales toward approval. In his testimony, Davidson told the House Health Subcommittee that Americans abroad are entitled to such health care benefits as a matter of simple justice, since they contribute through their taxes to the program. However, because of the rush to adjourn, the bill was not taken up by the Senate.

During the following year, a similar provision, S.-681, was introduced by Senators Abraham Ribicoff (D-CT), Patrick Moynihan (D-NY), Robert Dole (R-KS), and William S. Cohen (R-ME). The outlook was optimistic for the House bill, which was again sponsored by Rostenkowski. However, in February the Interstate and Foreign Commerce Committee killed the proposed legislation. Representative Phil Gramm (D-TX) said that he did not want the federal government "subsidizing Americans who live overseas." He was convinced that "the federal government should not provide further incentives for Americans to live abroad." Subcommittee Chairman Henry Waxman (D-CA) noted that some members felt that our citizens should not get the care at all if they leave the country. But, he added, "This is not a majority opinion."

Davidson thereupon flew to Washington to coordinate what he called an extensive educational campaign to persuade members of the committee to restore the provision to the bill. When Representative Gramm talked about costs, Davidson pointed out that the bill would not provide automatic coverage to Americans abroad but that coverage would be subject to bilateral agreements. HEW would stay within whatever budgetary limits were fixed. Gramm had no answer for that, but it didn't matter. He had convinced the committee, and this opposition killed the bill.

Addressing "Cinderella Citizenship"

While the Bipartisan Committee had focused on Medicare, the citizenship committees of AAWE and AARO were organizing a conference on American citizenship laws to be held on January 15, 1977. Plans called for a discussion by a panel of experts, followed by questions from the floor. The most knowledgeable American lawyer we knew for these matters was Russell Porter. Part of his youth had been spent in Paris, where his father had practiced international law. After serving with the U.S. Army during World War II, he had taken over his father's practice in France. He was active in the American Legion and Veterans of Foreign Wars posts in France and served as president of the American Overseas Memorial Day Association.[3] He agreed to present a summary of citizenship law as it applied to overseas residents.

The vice consul of the American Embassy, Gwen Coronway, agreed to answer questions. Helen Hootsman came from Amsterdam representing FAWCO. Becky Tan, now a permanent member of our team, came to Paris, traveling on her American passport.

We also invited Andrew Sundberg, whose letters to the editor of the *Tribune* criticizing citizenship laws had attracted our attention. Active with Democrats Abroad in Geneva, Sundberg was a graduate of the U.S. Naval Academy and Oxford University and had served in Vietnam.

He was married to a French citizen and worked as an economic consultant for American business groups in Switzerland. His two daughters had been born in Geneva and would have to reside in the United States for two consecutive years before age twenty-six in order to retain their U.S. citizenship. Sundberg called it "Cinderella citizenship." (By this phrase he meant that his daughters' citizenship was conditional on their residence in the United States for a specified period, just as Cinderella's attendance at the ball was conditional on her departure at midnight.)

Most of the work of organizing the conference fell to Kathleen de Carbuccia, who now headed both the AAWE and AARO citizenship committees. Originally from upstate New York, she had come to Paris on a foreign service assignment. After serving as vice consul in the embassy for two years, she had married a French publisher. Some years later, when her three children were old enough, she had enrolled in law school in France. After passing both the French and New York State bar examinations she joined an American law firm in Paris, Davis Polk & Wardwell.

Although the conference had been advertised, attendance estimated, and expenses calculated, there was—as always—a moment of worry before the designated hour. We surveyed the big room in the venerable Left Bank Hotel Lutetia, wondering whether there were too many of those delicate gilded chairs the French usually set up for meetings. Someone wondered whether they were solid enough to hold up those who appeared. But not everyone laughed. I for one took our self-appointed task very seriously. This was hard on Kathleen, who has a very optimistic nature. We made a good team.

In the end more than seventy people attended. Most of them came from France; but it was encouraging to greet attendees from Holland, Belgium, Switzerland, and Germany. Our field of action was moving beyond French borders. However, the majority of the attendees were women. I asked myself, where were the American fathers?

Russell Porter opened the meeting with a historical summary of American citizenship law. The main point of interest for those born overseas was that their citizenship is not protected by the Fourteenth Amendment to the Constitution. This amendment, passed shortly after the Civil War, was enacted to protect the citizenship of former slaves because it was feared that states would pass laws to limit their rights or deny their citizenship. It protects Americans "born or naturalized *in* the United States." Later in the afternoon Porter stated,

> If you read the Fourteenth Amendment literally, it says "born or naturalized in," and that apparently gives the Congress power to legislate this field, [power] it doesn't have for any other.

The ensuing discussion of the discriminatory nature of U.S. citizenship laws had some aspects of an encounter session. Attendees told their personal histories and expressed resentment that Americans living abroad are not always accorded the same rights as their fellow citizens in America. There were bitter complaints that the law differentiated between those born in the United States and those born abroad. For many, financial considerations such as health insurance coverage had determined the place of birth of their children. The situation of family members in the States was then and still is an important consideration. Other topics of discussion were registration of births at consulates and birth certificates, residence requirements of naturalized American citizens, problems of military service for dual nationals, travel with a foreign passport, renunciation of a foreign citizenship that had been acquired at birth, naturalization for children adopted overseas and problems of acquisition of a foreign nationality as an adult, usually for the purposes of employment.

Sundberg was an eloquent speaker and told the gathering that he had written to the White House and members of the Senate and House Judiciary Committees and had spoken with officials of the Justice Department about his daughters' situation. He fully intended to undertake further action in Washington.

The conference brought forth no definite plan of action, but it succeeded in establishing a bond between our organizations and key contacts from other European cities. When everyone had left, we sat down with Sundberg and discussed other laws and federal regulations that were unfair to Americans living overseas. We gave him the full picture of what AARO and AAWE had been doing to address these issues. Shortly thereafter, he founded his own organization in Geneva, calling it American Citizens Abroad (ACA).

On January 18, 1977, the *International Herald Tribune* published an article outlining the conclusions of the conference and our demands that Congress make changes in the Immigration and Nationality Act—not only the provisions affecting children born outside the United States, but also certain sections discriminating against naturalized citizens. The article noted that

> Participants also objected to the implication that Americans living abroad are "un-American," a view which they felt was often expressed in Washington. "The passport office seems to think that we are subversive Americans," grumbled an attendee. "They say we have left the country to escape military service and taxation." This brought a laugh from those who pay income tax to the United States as well as heavy taxes in the country where they reside.

The transcript of the conference ran to sixty pages. We had promised to distribute the report to participants, but we did not have the funds to pay for postage, let alone for printing the document. Just in time an American businessman living in Paris came to our aid and arranged to have 250 copies printed and bound. He was shocked and angry that his granddaughter, born in India, had been refused American citizenship. His daughter, who naturally had lived with him during his overseas assignments for the 3M Corporation, had married a citizen of India. She had not accumulated enough residence time in the United States to transmit citizenship to her child. This American grandfather had not been forewarned that serving American business interests overseas would carry such a penalty.

  Copies of the report were sent to the National Council of Women, the League of Women Voters, and the American Civil Liberties Union. A cover letter asked that they join us in our campaign to get these unfair laws off the books. There were no answers, not even an acknowledge-ment. Clearly, in this endeavor we could only count on ourselves.

Notes

1. See Appendix B.

2. At this writing, nineteen years later, Tan is active in American women's clubs in Germany, also serving as chair of FAWCO's citizenship committee and as general advisor to Americans on citizenship matters. In March 1995 she was elected President of FAWCO.

3. See Appendix A.

6

Going in Circles (1977-1978)

INCREASINGLY CONCERNED with provisions for retaining U.S. citizenship, Andrew Sundberg continued to write to Joshua Eilberg (D-PA), chairman of the House Immigration, Citizenship and International Law Subcommittee, asking him to introduce remedial legislation that would assure U.S. citizenship not only for his daughters but for all children born overseas of only one American-citizen parent. On a trip to Washington, Sundberg visited Eilberg's office every day until staff members finally arranged for him to meet with Eilberg personally. After Sundberg's explanations, Eilberg agreed to introduce legislation.

The bill (H.R.-9637), introduced on October 22, 1977, proposed to eliminate two sections of the law: section 301 (b), the two-year residence requirement applicable to children born overseas of one American parent only, and section 350, which provided that children of American parents who acquire dual nationality at birth can be automatically stripped of their U.S. citizenship if they live in the foreign country of which they are also a citizen for three consecutive years after reaching the age of twenty-two.

The Eilberg bill did not address the problem of transmission of citizenship. "Let's do this section first," he told

Sundberg, "and then we will get to the other sections during the next session of Congress." He improved the bill's prospects by asking Peter W. Rodino, Jr. (D-NJ), chairman of the House Judiciary Committee, to send the bill to the State and Justice Departments for their comments. Their approval would clear a major hurdle, because out of the thousands of bills that are introduced each year, only about 600 ever become law. If all the members of the subcommittee support the bill, it may go directly to the full committee without hearings. Sundberg was hoping that it would reach the floor of the House for a vote in April or May.

On November 15, 1977, Senator Kennedy introduced a companion bill with an additional proposal to amend the clause on the transmission of citizenship to a child born overseas of one American parent only. It would have reduced the physical residence requirement prior to the birth of the child from ten years to two.

In January 1978, our campaign for the passage of the Eilberg bill was launched with a second conference on citizenship, this time sponsored by an ad hoc group composed of the Republican and Democratic Party committees of Europe as well as ACA, FAWCO, AARO, AAWE, and FIAC.[1] Americans from England, Belgium, Holland, Germany, and Switzerland came to Paris for the event. Among them was Olivia de Havilland. Hoping to attract the attention of the American press, I asked her to speak with attendees and sit at the head table. She graciously agreed.

Another special guest was Angelika Schneider. In 1964 Schneider had challenged the power of Congress to expatriate naturalized citizens because they had elected to live outside the United States in their country of origin. She took her case to the Supreme Court and, as she said,

> After five years of litigation, court battles, and statelessness, 40,000 German marks of savings, and an unbelievable amount of dedicated, voluntary work by my lawyers in Washington, the law was declared unconstitutional.

She had won, and what is more, she had done it with no backing from any organization. The decision affirmed the phrase in the Fourteenth Amendment to the Constitution that protects the citizenship of anyone "born or naturalized *in* the United States." With this decision thousands of naturalized American citizens became free to live wherever they chose. That was exactly what we wanted for our children.

Samuel Gammon, minister-counselor for the American Embassy, opened the meeting by reading a special message from Assistant Secretary of State Barbara Watson, who congratulated us on our parental solicitude and patriotic zeal:

> You are to be highly commended for your active participation in the democratic process. You are right in striving to remedy any outmoded provision of law by taking direct action. I am pleased to inform you that the Department of State has replied to Peter Rodino of the House Judiciary Committee that we fully support the purpose of H.R.-9637 [the Eilberg bill] and recommend that its provisions be extended more broadly in order to specifically repeal all retention requirements. I commend you for your initiative in attempting to bring American law and policy governing citizenship matters into line with modern-day requirements.

We thanked the 3M Corporation for printing the analyses of the House and Senate bills to be sent to every member of Congress—535 pieces of mail. The best statement of the evening was Sundberg's: "The obligations of Americans abroad continue while abroad, but the benefits stop at the water's edge."

Addressing the Residence Requirement

In May 1978 Patricia Wald, the assistant attorney general, wrote to James Eastland (D-MS), chairman of the Senate Judiciary Committee, stating that the Justice Department favored the repeal of section 301 (b) on residence requirements for a child born abroad of one American parent only. She noted that "it has been difficult to administer and caused hardship in some situations. The Department suggests that all provisions relating to retention of U.S. citizenship should be repealed retroactively to May 24, 1934." On the subject of transmission of citizenship by an American parent (with foreign spouse) "the Department has no objections to a proposal to change the residence requirement, prior to the birth of the child, from ten years to two."

Her letter was a boon. It meant that the two federal agencies specifically chartered to administer citizenship law were on record as being in full agreement with our proposals for change. How could Congress ignore them?

On May 11, 1978, Americans staged a noisy demonstration outside the American Embassy in London. The next day a picture on the front page of the *International Herald Tribune* featured children waving banners with slogans such as "Children's Crusade for Fair Citizenship Laws," "I'm as American as Apple Pie," and "Don't Make Me Be Un-American."

An ACA press release dated May 10, 1978, contained several case histories. One of them dealt with the two-year residence requirement for retention of citizenship for a person born overseas of one American parent only. An American citizen who was attending graduate school in the United States and accomplishing the mandated two-year residence at the same time had been called back to Germany for his father's funeral. The proceedings took longer than the sixty-day absence allowed for "Cinderella citizens" who were fulfilling their statutory two years of residency. When he tried to return to America, he found that he had lost his American citizenship by overstaying the sixty days and, as he had no other nationality to fall back upon, had become stateless.

The second case had to do with transmission of U.S. citizenship to a child born abroad of only one American-citizen parent. An American woman who was married to a British citizen and living in London went to the American Embassy to register the birth of her fourth child. Her three other children had been issued U.S. passports upon her general recollection that she had lived in the United States ten years prior to their birth. This time, however, the consul asked her for the specific dates of her residence in America. When she provided the information, she discovered that she had been physically present in the United States for only nine years and two months and thus fell ten months short of meeting the previous residence requirement. The passports of the three older children were canceled, and the fourth child was denied U.S. citizenship.

Keeping up the pace of the campaign, a second conference on citizenship laws was sponsored that winter by the American Women's Club of Hamburg, Germany. The discussion was similar to that which had taken place at the Paris conference. The best question from the floor was, "What is citizenship anyway? A right, a privilege, or an emotional state of mind?"

Three New Laws

On October 5, 1978, as vice chairwoman of the Democratic Party committee in France, I wrote to Gerald Rafshoon at the White House. I recalled a lunch in Bonn the previous July with representatives of European Democratic Party committees, at which he had asked me what President Carter could do to obtain the votes of overseas Americans. My letter called his attention to three bills pending in Congress and suggested that it would help a great deal if all of them made it through Congress to the White House and received the President's signature. One was a new absentee voting bill that would prevent state legislatures from imposing taxes on the foreign-source income of overseas citizens who registered for a federal election absentee ballot. The second was the Eilberg citizenship bill. The third, a bill introduced by Senator George McGovern (D-SD), mandated a federal government study of its citizens resident abroad.

All three of these bills became law. The voting rights bill would permit many more Americans to vote absentee.

Under the law, an application for an absentee ballot was made to the last state of residence. In the majority of cases, the applicant did not own property, had no revenue from the state, and in some cases had not lived in the state for many years. Nevertheless, in reply to a request for an absentee ballot some county clerk offices were mailing tax forms. The new law would free overseas residents from this last stumbling block to the exercise of their right to vote.

The Eilberg citizenship bill, signed on October 10, 1978, eliminated the requirement that children born overseas of one American parent only must live continually in the United States for two years between the ages of fourteen and twenty-eight in order to retain their citizenship. This meant that the thousands of American children born overseas would no longer be second-class or "Cinderella citizens" at birth. The McGovern bill required the White House to identify all U.S. statutes and regulations that discriminate against overseas citizens and to recommend remedial action.

These new laws represented three major victories, but they were also steps in our ongoing campaigns, particularly with regard to citizenship law. The people and the structures of overseas groups were in place and determined to continue.

Congress had not acted on the recommendations it had received from Assistant Secretary of State Barbara Watson and Assistant Attorney General Patricia Wald. The Kennedy bill, which would have reduced the ten-year residence requirement to transmit citizenship, had gone nowhere. Furthermore, there was no provision to restore citizenship for those born between 1934 and 1952 who had lost it because of failure to reside for a required period of time in the United States. My own children were still denied reinstatement as U.S. citizens.

My son had registered for the draft in Washington shortly after his eighteenth birthday. In July 1970, during the Vietnam War, he reported to Robinson Barracks in Stuttgart, Germany, for a physical examination. He was classified 1A but was never called to active duty. He had planned to finish his MBA at San Francisco State College, but when his father suffered a serious illness my son was obliged to take his place in the family business in Paris. In so doing he lost the opportunity to study and live in America and, thus, to fulfill the residence requirement. Five years later, when preparing for a business trip to the United States, he went to the American Embassy to request renewal of his passport. It was refused. An employee of the passport office informed him that he was no longer what he had been all his life: a citizen of the United States. Nothing marked the occasion, and regrets were not expressed. He was advised to obtain a French passport and apply for a visa. Such was the way in which the United States rejected a young, competent French-American businessman engaged in transatlantic trade.

He joined his sister and the estimated 5,000 other people who had been stripped of their U.S. citizenship for failure to fulfill physical presence requirements that had been eliminated from the law in October 1978. What possible reason could have prompted Congress to vote against applying the law to them? It could not have been concern about the administrative paperwork it would entail; the Assistant Secretary of State herself had recommended retroactive application. Could it have been fear for the security of the United States? The thousands of visas issued to visitors each year negated that possibility. There was simply no logical answer.

The following month, our attention was drawn by congressional action on behalf of Russian dissidents. On November 16, 1978, the *Tribune* carried an article stating that "Twelve U.S. senators visiting Moscow asked the Kremlin for humane action and handed over a list of names and cases to Soviet authorities." The next day, I addressed a letter to the *Tribune's* editor, Murray Weiss, that was published on the editorial page on December 5, 1978.

> I see that the U.S. Congress continues to busy itself with Soviet citizens who wish to leave their country while ignoring U.S. citizens who wish the right to return to theirs. If

those who have lost U.S. citizenship or who are unable to transmit U.S. citizenship to their children will write to me, I will submit a list of their names and cases to these twelve U.S. senators who composed the delegation headed up by Senator Abe Ribicoff (D-CT).

On March 1, 1979, using the letterhead of the Citizenship Action Committee, Kathleen de Carbuccia and I addressed a letter to each of the twelve senators. Signing it as representatives of AARO and AAWE, we attached a copy of the International Bill of Human Rights.[2] Copies of the letter and accompanying documents went to Senator Kennedy; Peter Rodino (D-NJ), chairman of the House Judiciary Committee; Elizabeth Holtzman (D-NY), chairwoman of the House Immigration, Citizenship and International Law Subcommittee; and others.[3] In our letter we referred to the senators' concern for human rights and enclosed for their consideration four case histories of Americans resident overseas "who have fallen into difficulty with American citizenship laws." We wrote,

> While we realize full well that the problems of these people cannot compare in terms of daily hardship with those of Soviet citizens, they are nevertheless your fellow countrymen. They look to the U.S. Congress to ensure that American citizens and those of American parentage will not be deprived of their basic human rights. Liberalization of laws in other countries will only come about if America shows the way.

All of these people were, of course, known to the American consulate of their host country and had done whatever they could through those channels. They were caught between U.S. law and the laws of their country of residence. Their problems stemmed from section 349 (a): U.S. citizens risked the loss of their nationality by voluntarily "accepting employment under the government of a foreign state after attaining the age of eighteen, if [the U.S. citizen] has or acquires the nationality of the foreign state."[4] One woman, a professor at the University of Paris, had lost her citizenship because she had applied for and received French nationality. A divorced mother, she had taken this step in order to obtain tenure and increase her earnings. Another woman, a teacher in a French public school, feared the same consequence if she applied for French nationality. A third resided in Athens, where Greek nationality was required if one wished to work as a dentist in a public hospital. The official procedure in such cases was for the American citizen to first apply for and receive the foreign nationality; only then would the State Department decide whether the citizen had done so with the intention of renouncing American citizenship. The State Department would not give an advance ruling.

Still another woman's problem derived from a different prohibited action: "obtaining naturalization in a foreign state upon his own application, after having attained the age of eighteen years." She resided in Vienna and needed to establish eligibility in order to receive a government-paid pension in the event of her Austrian husband's death. Both she and the woman living in Greece had gone ahead and accepted the foreign citizenship, then waited in limbo for a decision from Washington. As in the case of Becky Tan, their "intention," their thoughts, were being examined from afar by employees of the State Department. Although this examination was based on affidavits that they themselves had written and submitted, they had no opportunity for a personal meeting with these officials unless they traveled to Washington. The names of the individuals making this all-important decision were not provided to them, nor did they have access to a transcript of the deliberations. They would not even be directly informed of the decision. The answer would be transmitted via the consular officer. The system was not hermetically closed to scrutiny, but the U.S. citizen who was defending his or her citizenship was hardly in a favored position.

On April 16, Representative Rodino acknowledged receipt of the letter and documents, saying that they had been referred to the House Immigration, Citizenship and International Law Subcommittee. On April 20, we received a letter from Stephan A. Dobrenchuk, director-designate of the Office of Citizens' Consular Services of the State Department. The two-page answer discussed how the State Department might come to a decision in such cases. It read in part as follows:

> The Department is willing to consider any evidence which has a bearing on the voluntariness of the act of expatriation. A person's responses to questions posed by a United States consular officer either in an interview or in various questionnaires, *the consular officer's opinion of the person's credibility,* and the significance and credibility of the evidence presented are important considerations in determining whether the presumption of voluntariness has been overcome. If it has been shown that the act was involuntary, expatriation will not occur.
>
> If the evidence presented establishes that an act as identified by the statute as expatriating was voluntarily performed, it becomes necessary to determine whether the act performed constituted a voluntary relinquishment of U.S. nationality as that term was used in the Afroyim decision and the Attorney General's opinion. In order to make such a determination, all the facts and circumstances of the case and the motives and purposes surrounding the commission of the act in question must be evaluated.

This letter and its formal language were discouraging. Were all of these opinions, determinations, and investigations really necessary? Did all of these factors have to be brought into play to appraise the conduct of two American women who wished to be teachers in France, another who wanted to work as a dentist in Greece, and a fourth who sought security for her old age? The choices made by these women couldn't possibly harm the United States. Must they really put their citizenship on the line for such commonplace reasons? America should be proud to have citizens who are capable of teaching in foreign schools and universities and working overseas as professionals. Every day, these people working in foreign countries show off the best qualities of our country.

Dobrenchuk addressed the four cases briefly in the last paragraph: "The individual case samples you enclosed with your letter are being forwarded to the appropriate foreign service posts for their comment and appropriate action." They were being sent back to the consular officers—back to square one. Representative Rodino had at least sent a referral letter, but we never heard from the twelve senators.

Talking it over, Kathleen and I reached the conclusion that the State Department was doing its best to administer an unjust and outdated provision of the law. All we could do was to continue to put pressure on Congress, even though improvement at some future date might be too late for the people whose lives had been damaged. Although it has been almost two decades, I will always wonder about the individuals who wrote to us describing their chagrin at the way their country was treating them and, for some, the real heartbreak at the loss of their country. We cared about each and every one of them.[5]

In January 1979, in response to a Freedom of Information request, we received figures on loss of citizenship over the past ten years from the Office of Overseas Citizens Services of the State Department. Under section 349 (a) (1) (obtaining naturalization in a foreign state upon personal application), there were 11,849 losses worldwide. Under section 349 (a) (4) (accepting, serving in, or performing duties of any office, post, or employment under the government of a foreign state after having acquired the nationality of such state), there were seventy-two losses.

Addressing Tax Issues

While all this was going on, efforts were also under way to combat unfavorable tax legislation. Although the Health and Human Services Administration and the State Department find it difficult to put overseas Americans on the same footing as those residing in the United States, the Internal Revenue Service has no such problem.

Americans residing overseas are required to file a return with the IRS just like other U.S. citizens. Their returns must include not only U.S. income but also *income earned overseas, on which they may have already been taxed by the host country.* It makes no difference whether their earnings were paid in local currency or in dollars or the nature or location of the employer: Americans were then (and are today) subject to the U.S. tax law on income of all types and sources anywhere in the world. Since tax laws for citizens of other industrial nations around the world also tax worldwide income for *residents* of their country, including income from U.S. sources, double taxation by two countries of the same income was (and is) a real and costly menace, despite international tax treaties and internal legislation designed to alleviate the problem.

The passage of the Tax Reform Act of 1976 was not good for the overseas American. It reduced the amount of the exemption overseas Americans could claim for income earned from foreign sources. This exemption was to compensate for the extra expenses of living overseas and the costs of moving, housing, school tuitions, and foreign sales (value-added) taxes, which are quite high in industrialized nations. The 1976 legislation cut the exemption back to $15,000. This action had serious implications and raised the consciousness of Americans overseas toward their government in Washington. It led to a tax petition addressed to Al Ullman (D-OR), chairman of the House Ways and Means Committee, and signed by 3000 members of American organizations overseas.

Nor was the tax law good for American foreign trade. The October 11, 1976, edition of *Business Week* called it an "unofficial foreign aid bill," claiming that

> The new legislation in the name of equal tax treatment for all U.S. citizens raises the cost of employing Americans abroad. It will hasten the replacement of U.S. expatriates by foreign nationals and widen the competitive edge foreign construction and drilling companies hold over U.S. concerns.

In November 1977, we received a letter from George E. Fischer of Irvine, California. His group, the American Constituency Overseas (ACO), focused on equitable tax treatment for oilmen and construction workers in remote areas of the Middle East, Africa, Southeast Asia, and the Far East. Fischer wrote,

> America is in deep trouble in the international business area. Current estimates place the 1977 balance of payments deficit at $30 billion. Part of the problem lies in the fact that the U.S. government, particularly Congress, has not understood the relationship between what Americans do overseas and the U.S. economy. Evidence of this was dramatically demonstrated when Congress amended section 911 of the U.S. Internal Revenue Code. Because of these changes American firms have been completely emasculated. As a result thousands of Americans will return stateside and thousands more at home will lose their jobs.

An article in an ACO newsletter noted that Americans overseas have positions of great influence even though they may not order American parts on a direct basis. It cited the role of the largely American faculty at the University of Petroleum and Minerals at Dhahran in Saudi Arabia. The university's graduates taught by Americans are inculcated with American products and systems. The article pointed out that "These young Saudis are destined to become the country's leaders and will remember what they were taught and who taught them."

The article stressed the hands-on competition taking place around the world:

> For Chevrolet, there is Volkswagon or Dodge (of England); for Caterpillar Tractor, there is Komatsu of Japan. These products are not purchased for price or quality alone. Export sales are often the result of familiarity and national loyalty. Those who design, specify and purchase tend to favor products from "home." The formula for increased export sales is simple: the more Americans working overseas, the greater export sales the U.S. can expect.

Some Bad News

Winding up a year in which we had worked on every issue and increased contacts with American groups elsewhere in the world, there came a bombshell. On December 13, 1977, Senator William A. Proxmire (D-WI) announced that he was giving his "Fleece of the Year" award

> to the U.S. Treasury Department for its zealous support of a last-minute, end of the year attempt to amend the tax laws. I am giving the award to the Treasury because they are pushing postponement for yet another year. They have succumbed to the moans from mink-swathed Americans abroad who now pay no or few taxes, but will have to begin paying, and to the arguments that the provision creates both jobs and stimulates business abroad.

This attitude was in total opposition to that of the French government toward French citizens living abroad, as voiced by Prime Minister Valéry Giscard d'Estaing when he spoke to the National Union of Overseas Frenchmen on July 6, 1977:

> It is clear that the future of France and the prosperity of the French people depend largely upon the capacity of our country to be present on the world scene and in major foreign markets. Frenchmen overseas assure with competence and dynamism this indispensable presence of France.

He announced a series of measures responding to "the demands of social justice that do not cease at the frontiers of our territory." He advocated better fiscal legislation, better social protection for salaried workers, the development of education possibilities for French children living overseas, and facilities for participation in all elections. He stated further that

> To all of you whom I know well and with whom I try to visit everywhere in the world, I send you today good news from France and transmit to you the affection of the large French family from which you must not feel separated because of distance.

About this time my daughter, who was engaged in research with the French National Scientific Research Center (CNRS), attended an international conference in Brussels. Noting her proficiency in English, an American scientist asked where she had learned to speak it so well. She answered that she had been brought up with both French and English, had gone to school in America, and had even worked for a short time for the U.S. Navy in Washington. She added that her mother was an American. "Oh," he said, "then you are an American citizen." "No," she replied, "I have lost my citizenship." She then explained briefly that she had not completed the required period of residence in the United States. "But how terrible!" he said. "You should get in touch with an American woman in Paris who has been working on problems of citizenship with a group of other Americans for a long time. If I can just remember her name, you can call her." "I know her name," said my daughter; "she is my mother."

Notes

1. See Appendix A.
2. Senators Abe Ribicoff (D-CT), Quentin N. Burdick (D-ND), Thomas Eagleton (D-MO), Adlai Stevenson, III (D-IL), Sam Nunn (D-GA), John Glenn (D-OH), Henry L. Bellmon (R-OK), Jacob Javits (R-NY), Robert Laxalt (R-NV), Lowell Schweiker (R-PA), John A. Durkin (D-NH), and Dennis DeConcini (D-AZ).
3. Barbara Watson and Brook Holmes, Bureau of Consular Affairs, Department of State; Anne Wexler, Office of Political Coordination in the White House; and James Reid, U.S. Consulate.
4. See Appendix B.
5. At the first world conference of Americans abroad, held in Paris on July 4, 1990, Carmen DiPlacido of the Overseas Citizens Service announced that those who had been stripped of their U.S. citizenship under section 349 (usually in order to hold a particular job in a foreign country) could request reinstatement as U.S. citizens by writing to the Department of State in Washington, D.C.

Signing of new protocol to Franco-American Tax Treaty, September 19, 1983.
From left: Stephanie Simonard, Association of American Residents Overseas; U.S. Ambassador Evan G. Galbraith; French Minister of Finance Jacques Delors; Charles Petrow, American Chamber of Commerce in France.

See p. 117

One Step Forward, Two Steps Back (1979–1982)

IN 1979 I began to look around me in a different fashion. My husband had retired and was playing a daily round of golf. Grandchildren, though a welcome joy, seemed to signal the arrival of a new stage of life. One Sunday afternoon, I found the popular song "It's My Turn" running through my thoughts. I decided then and there that I deserved a sabbatical. Six months later I was in Washington enjoying the hospitality of a dear friend and relative.

I had been active in the Democratic Party Committee in Paris and soon joined an informal group of Democrats who were former overseas residents. One of them was Martha Hartman, who had returned from Europe with a stong feeling for the problems confronting overseas residents and had become the Washington liaison for AARO. I had agreed to keep FAWCO informed of legislative action. At the time there were twenty member clubs representing some 7,000 women. Then as now, overhead costs were high, dues were low, and most activities and funds were directed toward the semiannual conference. My expense budget was $20.00 a year. Outlays were not excessive; they consisted of postage, photocopying, and transportation to congressional offices. Small sums add up, however, and in reply to a direct request several FAWCO clubs sent me checks; among them was a $100 donation from the American Women's League of Kuwait.

The second presidential election campaign since the federal postcard registration system had been established was under way, but overseas voters still faced many obstructions. We continued to hear complaints from Americans who had applied for absentee ballots and received them too late or not at all. Too many U.S. citizens were still disenfranchised by red tape.

Martha and Ursula Shears, another member of the group, undertook to write a series of letters to the offices of county clerks recommending that absentee ballots be mailed to voters abroad forty-five to sixty days in advance of Election Day with *airmail* postage. As a good Democrat, she also contacted the state Democratic Party chairs, explaining these difficulties and suggesting that there were votes to be garnered overseas.

The Federal Voting Assistance Program in the Department of Defense had been chosen to administer the new law. Martha and I visited their office in Arlington. The office was preparing a voting guide to disseminate information to overseas voters. It consisted of information such as the dates of primary elections, maps of states with congressional districts outlined, addresses of county clerk offices, descriptions of what is needed to obtain an absentee ballot, and copies of the federal postcard registration form. We gave the office a list of American nonprofit organizations to which the guide could be mailed when it became available.

Focusing on Citizenship

During this activity on behalf of absentee voters, our concern with citizenship laws was not forgotten. In the fall of 1979 Martha and I held two meetings with Ruth McLendon, deputy assistant secretary for overseas citizens services of the Bureau of Consular Affairs at the State Department. She introduced us to Carmen DiPlacido of the bureau's European Services Division. I brought up the case histories of American women we had earlier submitted to the twelve senators (see Chapter 6). He reassured us and said that the State Department will always look into a case and that if there is any doubt about about the individual's intention to renounce U.S. citizenship the Department will rule in the person's favor. Furthermore, under the Freedom of Information Act, people who are informed that they have lost their U.S. citizenship may ask to see the telegram the bureau has sent to the consulate giving the reasoning for the decision. Those who believe the action is unfair may ask for an administrative review, which is conducted by the Bureau of Consular Affairs, or may appeal to the review board. The individual who takes such action has the right to a temporary passport in order to come to Washington to appear before the board. If the board's ruling is unfavorable, the applicant can go to the district court, where the case is opened anew.

DiPlacido told us that pursuant to legislation introduced by Senator Kennedy in 1979, Congress had appointed a Select Commission on Immigration and Refugee Policy—"a national committee established to provide a comprehensive review for immigration and refugee laws, policies, and procedures."

Members of the commission included four cabinet members, four members each from the Senate and House Judiciary Committees, and four presidential appointees, including the chairman, who happened to be the president of Notre Dame University.

On October 18, 1979, Martha and I met with two staff members of the commission, Charles Smith and Mary Jo Gratenrath, and explained the situation of Americans overseas in depth. We submitted case histories detailing some of the hardships that were being caused by the citizenship laws. We recommended (1) that the ten-year previous residence requirement for transmission of citizenship to a child born overseas of only one American parent be reduced to two years; (2) that citizenship be restored to the approximately 5,000 persons born between 1934 and 1952 who had been deprived of their citizenship for failure to reside in the United States for a requisite period (on the basis of the law since amended); and (3) that the provision providing for loss of citizenship upon acquisition of a second nationality in order to accept employment with a foreign government be rescinded. We explained that in many foreign countries occupations that have nothing to do with the policymaking aspects of government fall under the heading of "government employment." These include jobs in nationalized industries such as commercial aviation, railroads, banks, schools, and even libraries or museums.

Shortly thereafter we met with Andrew J. Carmichael, acting associate commissioner of the Immigration and Naturalization Service (INS). It was important to know his outlook on these questions and to make him realize the difficulties they created. We again outlined our position, particularly with regard to the problem of employment overseas. We explained that Americans were teaching English in public secondary and graduate-level schools and that French universities often assigned readings from American textbooks still in their original English versions. The special tutoring in English offered to French students was very often provided by U.S. citizens. In these positions Americans were not only teaching English but aiding in the distribution of works by American scholars. The United States Information Agency sent its foreign service employees overseas to do exactly the same thing. Where was the difference?

Carmichael emphasized that while other countries' laws limiting the rights of U.S. citizens remained inflexible, the United States had almost completely eased its work restrictions on resident aliens. He felt that instead of expecting the United States to adapt its laws, overseas Americans should try to get other countries to amend theirs. Nevertheless, he held open the possibility of change in U.S. laws and urged Martha to appear at a regional public hearing of the Select Commission in New York City.

In January 1980 Martha went to New York and testified for AARO on behalf of all overseas citizens. She stated that both she and her husband were native-born Americans and had lived both in France and in Belgium, where her husband was a correspondent for Associated Press. Their daughter had been born in the United States, but owing to her father's employment overseas she had been raised overseas with them. She had, however, attended American schools in Belgium and lived in the United States for four consecutive years while attending college. She was married to a French citizen and would like to have a child. She wanted this child to be an American citizen. But as she had not completed ten years of residence (five after the age of fourteen) in the United States, she could transmit American citizenship to her child only if she left her husband, assuming that she could afford to do so, and went to the States for the birth of the child. As parents the Hartmans had not been in a position to send their daughter to live in the United States without them, at least not until she reached a relatively mature age. Nor could the daughter, as a minor, choose where to live. Now the daughter could hardly be expected to leave her husband in order to live in the States to complete the requisite number of years. Thousands of U.S. citizen parents who had been brought up abroad faced this painful dilemma. For this reason, AARO was urging elimination of the remaining vestiges of discrimination against American citizens.

Winding up her work at the Select Commission, Gratenrath informed me that an intensive review of the issues was to be carried out by a small group to draft legislative proposals. Accordingly, we prepared a three-page document describing our position and including a copy of a letter from the Justice Department, which in 1979 had no objection to reducing the required residence period for transmission of citizenship by an American-citizen parent married to a foreign national from ten years to two. We pointed out once more that transmission was often denied because of the parent's residence overseas during childhood, when he or she had no control over the family's place of residence. We also noted that the law made an exception for those who had lived overseas as minor children of employees of the federal government, the armed forces or an international government organization. We believed that the same policy should apply to all American citizen parents living overseas.

Finally, we asked that the law be modified so as to prevent statelessness for children of American parentage born overseas. The cases of two stateless children who had been born in Belgium were presented by Kathy Webster, an American woman living in Brussels. Each child had a Belgian mother and an American father, neither of whom could transmit citizenship to the child. Belgian law did not permit transmission by its female citizens.[1] Nor did it automatically confer citizenship upon all who were born within its borders. The American fathers could not transmit U.S. citizenship because of lack of sufficient residence in the U.S. prior to their birth. We cited article 15 of the International Bill of Human Rights: "Everyone has the right to a nationality."

Among others who addressed letters to the Select Commission was ACA's Andrew Sundberg, who said in part,

> We do not believe that American children born abroad constitute a threat to the United States. We do believe that the continued obstinate refusal to recognize the human rights of its own children abroad constitutes a grave threat to the credibility of our commitment to the human rights of all of the inhabitants of the world.

Senator Kennedy had introduced a bill that contained an amendment to the transmission clause reducing the residence period from ten years to two. Martha checked the progress of the bill periodically. Her notes tell a sad story:

> Feb 19, 1980: No progress, committee [Senate Immigration and Refugee Subcommittee] busy with refugee bill.
>
> April 11: A meeting scheduled to consider our amendment.
>
> April 28: The committee met, but did not have a quorum, so nothing was accomplished on our amendment.

May 16: The bill with our amendment will come up at the next meeting on May 20.

May 28: Committee met, but did not get to the bill.

June 4: Bill still not in shape, no one is against our provision, but it takes time.

July 9: Bill is reported out of committee with our revision.

August 7: Bill is reported out and on Senate calendar; but no date is set, no futher action possible until after the recess for the Democratic Convention.

September 8: Bill not yet scheduled; perhaps later in the week.

January 1981: Meeting with Jerry Tinker [of the subcommittee staff], no definite action on the citizenship bill.

There were other contacts with Senator Kennedy's office and members of the House Judiciary Committee. I met with Representative Hamilton Fish, Jr. (R-NY). Representative Robert McClory (R-IL) took a personal interest in our proposals because his daughter was married to a Swiss citizen and lived in Geneva with her Swiss-born children. It was through him that our committee met Eugene Pugliese, the legal counsel of the House Judiciary Committee. Little did we know that we would be calling upon him for action on citizenship laws for the next fifteen years. At our last meeting he was as patient as ever, with a comprehensive attitude toward the serious problems these laws engender but also very aware of the complications of the legislative process itself.

In March 1981 the final report of the select commission was finally published and sent to Congress. Finding that "the present ten-year requirement is unduly restrictive in the world of modern travel and places an inordinate burden on some U.S. citizens," it recommended two-year prior residence for transmission of citizenship to a child born abroad of one American and one foreign national, *except* that any period the citizen parent had been physically present abroad as the dependent unmarried son or daughter and member of the household of a person

honorably serving with the armed forces of the United
States or employed by the U.S. government or an international organization may be included in order to satisfy the
physical residence requirement.

The decision was very liberal. The recommendation
to reduce the residence requirement from ten years to two
would be a great improvement. On the other hand, the
inequity of the law was confirmed in that a clear distinction was made between people employed by the federal
government overseas and people living overseas for any
other reason. In addition, the commission recommended
that "those whose citizenship was lost solely by reason of
failure to reside in the United States under any prior law
shall be deemed to be restored to their citizenship status
as of the date of such loss." This once more raised my hopes
that American citizenship would be returned to the 5,000
former citizens, including my children, whose status was
unaffected by the 1978 amendment.

"Ask Michael"

We had been relatively successful in convincing the members of the commission. Now we had to turn once more to
Congress to make the commission's recommendations a
reality. But we felt that there was reason for optimism.

In January 1981 Judith Bingham of Republicans
Abroad in Paris had received a telegram from President
Ronald Reagan that stated in part: "I want to thank you
for your help, your assistance in the recent election and
assure you that my administration is aware of the problems of Americans living abroad and that we intend to
address these problems at an early date."

Kathleen de Carbuccia had turned over the direction of the citizenship committees of both AAWE and
AARO to Michael Adler. A native of Baltimore, Michael
had received her degree in law from George Washington
University and then worked for seven years as a legislative analyst for the National Institutes of Health in

Bethesda, Maryland. Upon her marriage to a French academic she moved to Paris. She quickly identified with the difficulties of citizenship laws and gradually became the person to whom people with citizenship problems were referred. "Ask Michael" became a familiar phrase. It was she who first met Arnold H. Leibowitz, a special counsel to Alan Simpson (R-WY), chairman of the Senate Judiciary Committee. He was, like Pugliese on the House side, an important person for our cause.

In September 1981, Michael, Martha, and I talked with Leibowitz and were told that both Peter Rodino (D-NJ), chairman of the House Judiciary Committee, and Romano Mazzoli (D-KY), chairman of the House Subcommittee on Immigration, International Law and Refugees, needed to be convinced of the real need for amendments to the law. Their hesitation was rooted in the fear that the changes we advocated would open the doors to people who had no real ties to the United States. We explained that those for whom we spoke were voters and taxpayers and that their children attended American schools both in the United States and abroad. They traveled frequently to the States for business or pleasure and often visited relatives and friends who lived in the United States. In fact, those friends and relatives often turned up in the U.S. citizens' host countries as tourists and sometimes as residents. In short, there were many more opportunities to maintain ties with America than there had been, for example, in the years immediately following World War II.

The INS came back into the picture with a letter to Andrew Sundberg from the acting associate commissioner, Andrew J. Carmichael. His letter included the statement that "Pressing issues of refugees and illegal immigration inevitably eclipse the relatively noncontroversial citizenship issues." He said that an interagency task force was studying the commission's recommendations.

Shortly thereafter, I learned that the interagency task force's report did not deal with our problems and, worse, that the report would go to the president for his signature within a week. The citizenship problems of American children born overseas had been passed over in favor of those of illegal immigrants. David Hiller, special assistant to the attorney general, offered to submit our case directly to the task force, suggesting that we prepare a three-page summary of the citizenship problems, including case histories, and deliver it to him within ten days.

Once more we were off and running. Michael prepared the basic document, which we had typed on a joint letterhead of AAWE, AARO, and FAWCO. An acknowledgment from Hiller stated that the file had been recommended to the acting commissioner of the INS for comments and assured us that our views would be taken into consideration.

We had our answer two months later in a letter from the acting commissioner, Doris M. Meissner. Commenting on why there had been no action on our proposals, she used Carmichael's exact phrasing: "Pressing issues of refugees and illegal immigration have inevitably eclipsed the relatively noncontroversial citizenship issues."

I responded,

> While we fully understand the pressing needs of refugees and the very serious problems raised by the large numbers of illegal aliens in America, this priority does not eliminate the hardship and heartbreak suffered by some American citizens born and raised in this country.

And so it went during 1981—as it had in 1980 and would in 1982. Our letters, proposals, telephone contacts, meetings, and communications from individuals and organizations to House and Senate committees and to the State and Justice Departments all led nowhere.

Notes

1. This law was repealed in 1985. The new law permits transmission of citizenship through a female married to a non-Belgian.

Another Partial Victory (1982–1987)

IN THE fall of 1978 President Jimmy Carter signed legislation introduced by Senator George McGovern (D-SD) that mandated a study of the nation's treatment of its citizens resident overseas. The objective was to identify all U.S. statutes and regulations that discriminate against such citizens and to recommend remedial action by legislation or any other appropriate measures. Robert Lipschutz, counsel to President Carter, was named to carry out the study. Organizations representing overseas citizens all submitted reports drawn from statements by individual Americans. American Citizens Abroad (ACA) delivered its compilation directly to Secretary of State Cyrus Vance during an official trip he made to Geneva. The final report was delivered to Senator Frank Church, chairman of the Foreign Relations Committee, on July 2, 1980. It described sixty-three discriminatory laws and regulations in the areas of citizenship, social security, taxation, veterans' rights, and the education of children overseas. This was the first time that all of these issues had been brought together in one document. However, knowing that it would be a long time before any positive results would come about through this compendium, overseas groups continued their reform efforts, especially in the area of taxation.

Tax Relief for Overseas Americans

By December 1980 lobbying efforts had led to legislation to reduce the tax burden on American citizens abroad. The President's Export Council adopted a report by its Export Expansion Subcommittee recommending tax laws that would put Americans working overseas on the same tax footing as citizens from competing industrial nations. Tax relief for overseas Americans was the subject of hearings before the House Ways and Means Committee on April 7, 1981. Robert T. Angarola, an attorney praticing in Washington, testified on behalf of ACA. He stated that

> The reduction of the foreign source income tax credit has had a very negative effect on our export performance. From 1926 to 1962 the U.S. government did not tax foreign earned income. This was due primarly to a recognition of the benefits derived from having Americans overseas who would not only bolster our commerical standing in the world, but also transmit our social and economic ideology to other peoples. We correctly believed that the most effective means of convincing people that the American way of life and the American form of government were the best models to follow was to have our citizens live and work in foreign lands.

> Because of a few isolated instances of wealthy overseas Americans taking advantage of existing loopholes in the tax law and actively avoiding their responsibilities as citizens, in 1962 our tax policy changed. The actions of these individuals gave Americans living in the United States an impression that every American abroad owned limousines and wore mink coats, and resided on the shores of the Mediterranean. This stereotype is of course far from reality. The small businessman trying to establish a market in a West African country, the construction engineer working in the Mid-East desert, or the low-salaried teacher struggling to survive in an expensive European city bear little resemblance to this image of affluence.

> Our tax policy has made it more and more difficult for Americans to live abroad. In addition to the impact this has had on exports, it has driven out of foreign countries the very people we need to transfer our ideals to citizens of other

nations. We are a country built upon the tradition of the "Yankee trader," the entrepreneurial capitalist who through his own efforts makes a better life for himself, his family, and his society. This is the capitalist system at its best, a system we have attempted at great expense to have other nations adopt. Our present tax policy is thwarting this effort.

White House Liaison

Alfred E. Davidson, still an active member of the AARO board, was convinced that overseas Americans should now turn to the White House for redress. He conferred with our good friend Eugene Marans in Washington and also enlisted the aid of Ambassador Edwin M. Martin of the Population Crisis Committee. Accordingly, in July 1984 a bipartisan effort was initiated by way of a petition to the White House requesting the nomination of a presidential advisor for the affairs of overseas Americans. Marans and Martin then met with presidential aide Franklin Lavin. The White House reacted quickly and on August 16 named Douglas A. Riggs to the newly created position of special advisor for the affairs of overseas Americans. Riggs was to help formulate White House policy, particularly with a review of proposed legislation submitted to the office of the president. It was hoped that the post would become a permanent one and lead to a new channel of influence on Congress, but it was difficult to use the privilege effectively from overseas. A permanent representative in Washington was needed to brief the advisor periodically. In the absence of that kind of follow-up, the initiative was not successful.

Our citizenship committee followed these parallel efforts but continued to focus primarily on an immigration reform bill introduced in March 1982. Arnold Leibowitz advised us that as drafted in the Senate subcommittee, the bill would reduce the ten-year prior residence period for transmission of citizenship by an American parent with a foreign-citizen spouse to a child born abroad to two years after the age of fourteen. He told us that Senator Simpson would go along with the opinion of his staff,

which was sympathetic to our cause. Opposition would
come from the House.

I felt that I had to try to convince Romano Mazzoli
(D-KY), chairman of the House Subcommittee on Immigration, International Law and Refugees, that the proposed
changes were justified by the circumstances that stemmed
from working overseas. After calling his office several times,
I was able to get an appointment on June 28. As I expected
the question of taxation to come up, I asked Robert
Angarola to accompany me.

Representative Mazzoli was extremely negative, expressing opinions similar to Senator Proxmire's assertions
against Americans abroad who did not pay taxes. Angarola
explained that overseas residents were taxpayers and that
they often paid taxes twice—to their host country and to
the United States. He pointed out that the roughly 3 million overseas residents couldn't *all* be millionnaires, that
there had to be some who were bona fide middle-class tax-
paying citizens trying to make a living. When the discussion turned to working overseas, I brought up section 349
of the Immigration and Nationality Act, which dealt with
the acquisition of a foreign nationality in order to comply
with the host country's employment laws. At that point
Mazzoli became antagonistic, saying that if people took
on a second nationality they should stay in that country.
What would his constituents in Kentucky think if they knew
he was in favor of U.S. citizens working overseas? He qui-
eted down, though, and conceded that he had played the
role of devil's advocate. It all ended peacefully, and he
promised to read the legislative proposals prepared by
Michael Adler that I left with him.

Four years later the State Department sponsored the
Immigration and Nationality Act Amendments of 1986.
In January Kathleen de Carbuccia, Michael Adler, Maureen
Coots (from Brussels), Roberta Enschede[1] (from Amsterdam),
Erica Parra, and Andrew Sundberg (from Geneva) met in
Paris to discuss how best to work for a favorable congres-
sional vote. Enschede had 2,000 postcards printed with an
illustration of Santa Claus handing a U.S. passport to a

child with an American flag. They were distributed through FAWCO clubs. The result was over 600 letters and cards sent to the House subcommittee.

At congressional hearings held on August 11, 1986, Arnold Leibowitz, who by then had left Congress for private practice, testified for ACA, FAWCO, and AARO, collectively representing over 30,000 American citizens resident overseas. He presented fourteen case histories relating to transmission of U.S. citizenship to children of American parentage born abroad. Two of them involved American military personnel. In one of these cases, a child had been born in an American military hospital in Germany. The little girl had been denied U.S. citizenship because her American mother had not lived in the United States long enough to transmit citizenship while her father, a resident alien serving in the U.S. Army, could not transmit citizenship either. The child was therefore stateless. The mother had come to Germany to join her husband on a command-sponsored tour eight months before her nineteenth birthday. A *Stars and Stripes* article submitted as testimony quotes the mother:

> Following the advice of the American consul, I asked the German government for a passport, since the girl was born in Germany. They (the German authorities) almost laughed me out of the office. They said I was American and my daughter was born in an American hospital, so there was no way they could grant citizenship.

The American consulate told her that once the family was back in the United States there would be no problem—the child could be naturalized quickly. However, when the mother applied for an immigration visa she was told that she couldn't get one because the child didn't have a passport from any country. This case undoubtedly may be classed as an administrative snafu, but it must have been traumatic for a young mother and father.

The second military case concerned Master Sergeant Leroy Barnes, who died in combat in Vietnam in 1966. He was awarded two Purple Hearts, several Army

Commendation Medals, a Presidential Citation, and the Air Medal. But his grandchildren are not Americans. Barnes, born in the United States, joined the Army in his twenties and became a professional soldier. During an overseas assignment he met and married a native of Switzerland who was naturalized as a U.S. citizen in 1956. Following his death in 1966, she took her three children to live with her family in Switzerland. The oldest of the three, Anne Laraine (born in the United States), married a Swiss citizen and had four daughters. None of them can be U.S. citizens. Anne Laraine lived for seventeen and a half years as an army dependent, more than meeting the ten-year prior residence requirement. But the law requires that five of those ten years must be after the age of fourteen. She could not fulfill this provision. The ACA summary of this case stated that

> Her father had died too soon. Sergeant Barnes's government has publicly expressed its gratitude for his having given his life on behalf of all of the citizens of the United States. The State Department has also written many letters to Sergeant Barnes's daughter to explain why they won't acknowledge her children as citizens of the United States. Sergeant Barnes died for real Americans. His government says that they do not include his own grandchildren.

The following case history was prepared for the subcommittee by Kathy Webster, a resident of Brussels whose grandchildren have been denied U.S. citizenship. It calls attention once more to the price businesspeople may pay for their overseas careers.

> Both my husband and myself were born, raised, educated in the United States and both have ancestral ties that go back to pre-Revolutionary days. My husband is a lawyer with a U.S. firm and has spent all but four of his thirty years of practice in their overseas office, serving U.S. corporate interests abroad. Our four daughters have consequently been brought up mainly living with their family in Europe. But they lived for four years in New York and returned frequently to the U.S. for long holiday trips, summer school at the Phillips Exeter Academy and for their college education at

Wellesley College. Two of the girls chose French husbands and are currently living in Europe. One teaches English and American studies in a bilingual school near Paris, the other works as registration supervisor in the agricultural products department of a large American company. They now have five children between them to whom they could not transmit their U.S. nationality because they did not complete the ten-year residence in the U.S.A. One of the daughters had arranged to return to the U.S. to give birth, in spite of the enormous expense involved. She unfortunately became diabetic and could not be moved, and was so upset she almost lost her baby. When the other daughter flew to the U.S. with her family for vacation there, the full trauma of the fact that she was American, but her children were not, struck her a hard blow, as she was separated from them at the point of entry.

At international arrival terminals passengers are divided into two lines: citizens and aliens. This undoubtedly makes for quicker processing of the hundreds of passengers who arrive daily, but it comes as a shock for American parents who are unable to shepherd their children or grandchildren through immigration control. As one frustrated young mother described it,

Having to apply for a visa every time we visit my family in the United States, filling out forms certifying that my four-year-old daughter isn't a communist, drug user, or importer of pornographic literature! I find this situation nonsensical and outrageous. The law concerning transmission must be changed. After all, I did not choose to leave America before completing ten years' residence there, so why should my children be victimized by circumstances entirely out of my control?

Changes in the Citizenship Law

With a new name, the Citizenship Reform Act of 1986 became law with the signature of President Reagan on November 14, 1986. Finally, five years after the Select Commission had made its recommendations, the requirements for transmission of citizenship were reduced. The U.S. residency requirement (section 301 (g)) for transmitting U.S. citizenship to children born abroad of one U.S.-citizen parent and one foreign-citizen parent was reduced to five years (two after age fourteen) from ten (five after age fourteen). Although overseas groups all over Europe had worked vigorously to have this requirement reduced to a simple two years in the aggregate, to be applied retroactively to include children who were under age eighteen at the time of the law's passage, Congress was unwilling to go that far.

There were other positive changes. Naturalized U.S. citizens could now leave the country one year after naturalization without raising the presumption that they did not intend to reside in the United States when they acquired citizenship. Prior to this amendment, such citizens had to reside in the United States five years after naturalization to avoid risking revocation.

The new law abolished entirely the requirement that an American child who obtained foreign nationality upon a parent's application must go to the United States with the intention of establishing permanent residence prior to his or her twenty-fifth birthday in order not to lose U.S. citizenship. The law also eased the situation of U.S. citizens who obtain a foreign nationality in order to hold a particular job in a foreign country. The automatic presumption of intent to relinquish U.S. citizenship was abandoned; the burden of proof of such intent was shifted to the State Department.

The new law gave textual legislative weight to what federal courts had been requiring for over a decade. That is, in order to take away a U.S. citizen's nationality for performing certain proscribed acts (among them obtaining naturalization in a foreign state) the State Department had to prove that the individual had done so with the actual intention of relinquishing U.S. citizenship.

But there was still no redress for the 5,000 persons not covered by the 1978 amendment. It gave amnesty to thousands of illegal immigrants living in the United States, but not to children born overseas of American parents.[2]

Angry and frustrated, I imagined a final verse to the Emma Lazarus poem inscribed on the Statue of Liberty:

As I welcome the poor and the hungry
So will I take these five thousand well fed.
To them all without bias,
I open the golden door.

However, little by little we were changing the law, and as we progressed, the need to inform overseas citizens grew. The best format was still public discussion, usually in the form of a meeting organized by an American group. In February 1987 a Citizenship Information Session was held in Germany. It was sponsored by the American Women's Club of Hamburg, led by Carol Battenfeld. The consul and vice consul of the American Consulate were present. The discussion was tape recorded and a verbatim report printed and distributed. The following excerpts taken from the transcript are a good example of a very unfortunate state of mind.

Vice-Consul Eric Sandberg, commenting on the new citizenship law reducing the residence period for transmission of U.S. citizenship to a child born overseas of one American parent only, explained that physical presence in the United States can also include time spent outside the country as the dependent of an active-duty military person or an employee of the federal government or certain international organizations. The transcript of his remarks reads, in part, as follows:

Sandberg: So that residence overseas as a dependent counts as physical presence because you were out there for a "good purpose." We aren't going to penalize you. They don't penalize us. For example, my children, while they are here in Hamburg a year and a half, that time counts as physical presence in the U.S.

Battenfeld: By what means do they decide what an American company is? We know a particular case where it was an American company but...

Sandberg: It is not just an American company. It has to be governmental either for the federal government itself, or for certain international organizations, like the United Nations.

Battenfeld: I see.

Sandberg: U.N. organizations count.

Battenfeld: International Harvester isn't what they mean?

Sandberg: No. Not a private organization.

This exception to the law, this privilege for federal employees, civilian and military, clearly is basically unfair to private sector American employees overseas and leads to a ludicrous basis for bestowing American citizenship on an infant born overseas of only one American parent. Under this law, the determining factor may someday be the employer of the infant's grandparent.

Consider Baby A and Baby B, who are born in a foreign country of an American father and a foreign-citizen mother. Baby A's American father, who was born in the United States, spent some, but not all, of his formative years abroad as his father worked overseas for an agency of the U.S. government. He had attended American schools in the United States and abroad, knew all about George Washington, loved Oreo cookies, voted in U.S. elections, and paid his taxes on April 15. Employed by an American bank in Rome, he married an Italian citizen and they were blessed with Baby A. Even though the father had not lived in the United States for the total number of years required by the law, the baby was duly registered as an American citizen by the consulate. Happily, the years the father had spent abroad as the dependent of a federal employee counted as residence in the United States. A good thing for Baby A that his grandfather had been in the foreign service.

Now take Baby B. His American father, born in the United States, also spent some, but not enough, of his formative years overseas; his father was an export sales agent for American manufacturers of, say, spigots, faucets, machine tools, *Star Trek* reruns, Barbie dolls, or oil drilling equipment. This American parent also attended American schools both at home and abroad, spent summer vacations with his grandparents in the States, and often dined on peanut butter and jelly sandwiches. Later, as a professor of American history at the American University of Paris, he taught his pupils all about George Washington. He voted in U.S. elections and paid his taxes on time. He married a British citizen. Baby B was born in Paris. But unlike Baby A, Baby B will be denied U.S. citizenship because her grandfather chose to earn his living working for American business interests—not a "good reason" for living abroad, according to Vice-Consul Sandberg. Thus does the identity of the the grandfather's employer determine whether some children may gain the protection of American citizenship while others are rejected.

It is impossible for parents to foresee or control whom their children will marry or where their future grandchildren will be born. But under the law, if Americans choose to work in the private sector overseas, they may effectively endanger the U.S. citizenship of those future grandchildren.

Notes

1. Enschede is active with the American Community Council in Holland, which sponsors the annual Thanksgiving Day celebration in the Pieterskerk church in Leiden where the Minister to the Pilgrims is buried. When Representatives Bill Alexander (D-AR) and Benjamin A. Gilman (R-NY) cosponsored a House Joint Resolution declaring April 19 Dutch-American Friendship Day, it was as a result of Enschede's efforts.
2. Nearly 1.4 million illegal aliens met the May 4, 1988, the deadline for applying for amnesty under the Immigration and Naturalization Act *(World Almanac 1995).*

Progress on All Fronts
(1988–1990)

As AARO entered its second decade, its membership stood at 600 people in twenty-seven countries. Its president was Stephanie Simonard, a native of Washington, D.C. She had studied political economics during her college year abroad, where she met the Frenchman who became her husband. As a senior tax manager and then partner with a prominent international accounting firm, she had firsthand experience with the burdens of taxation that faced American businesspeople in France. She brought that knowledge to both French and American tax administrators as they negotiated a new protocol to the French-American tax treaty to reduce double taxation between the two countries, and she was invited to be present at the signing of the protocol on September 19, 1983. *seo p94*

A second French-American agreement, this time on Social Security, was signed three years later. Considering this agreement very important for American business, Ambassador Joe Rodgers had made finalization of this treaty a top priority. It allows individuals to include their total years of employment in both countries in calculating their entitlement to pension benefits.

When an American company sets up an overseas subsidiary, whether it is a manufacturing facility or an import firm, the company is a legal entity of the host country. As such, all employees, including U.S. citizens, contribute to the host country's social security administration and are entitled to whatever benefits are paid to workers, including pension rights. If the U.S. employee was paid in dollars, that employee was also obligated to contribute to the U.S. Social Security system. Thus more and more Americans found themselves paying into two systems. Foreign citizens employed by foreign subsidiary companies in the United States were faced with the same situation. As a general rule, these international employees, who spent an average of two to five years away from their homeland, did not contribute for a long enough period to receive full benefits upon retirement. Their contributions thus were lost.

The history of these bilateral accords began in 1977 with legislation authorizing U.S. diplomatic representatives to reach agreements with other nations on Social Security payments and benefits. The problems of double taxation and double coverage were patiently worked out, country by country, by the administrative staffs of the governments concerned. As of 1995, these so-called totalization agreements have been reached with seventeen countries.[1]

There was a short-lived attempt by the Reagan administration to limit this program, but these efforts were halted when the General Accounting Office reported that more money was coming into the United States in the form of pension income through these accords than was being paid out.

Health Care Solutions

In response to many requests, AARO began to explore the feasibility of developing a group health insurance plan for its members. Many Americans who retire abroad have lived and worked overseas and as a consequence are covered by the government-funded health care system of their host country. There is a special problem for retired professionals and military personnel; they are covered by CHAMPUS (Civilian Health and Medical Program of the Uniformed Services), which is administered by the Defense Department. They lose their protection at age sixty-five, the assumption being that Medicare will take over. But as overseas residents they end up with no coverage and are usually too old and without adequate income to qualify for an individual policy with Blue Cross/Blue Shield or other companies.

Not all Americans living overseas can afford the high premiums and hence lack medical insurance. In 1984 an AARO member, Leo E. Packer, agreed to find a solution. He had retired in Paris after a career in government service, notably as director of technology policy and space affairs in the State Department. For almost two years he discussed his "ideal" plan with insurance brokers and underwriters without generating much interest. The organization was too small and there were no statistical data to define the insured population. Finally he located a company that agreed to underwrite a plan close to his original concept, which went into operation in 1986. ACA in Geneva has a comparable program for its members. In the absence of Medicare benefits these insurance plans are of real service to American retirees who live abroad.

The English-Language Press Overseas

Joining other American publications such as the *Wall Street Journal, Newsweek, Time,* and *Reader's Digest, USA Today* had launched its European and Asian editions in 1985. These were first distributed in thirty-three countries in Europe and the Middle East and twelve countries in Asia and the Pacific. The following year *USA Today* became the only U.S.-based publication to begin systematic coverage of overseas Americans themselves. A special column headlined "USA Abroad," published semiweekly, describes the lives of individuals and the activities of nonprofit institutions, churches, and schools; and reports legislative news of special interest to them. At present the international edition is sold in ninety-nine countries. Average daily sales have tripled to 75,000; 53,000 are sold in Europe and the Middle East and 22,000 in Asia. A 1994 survey showed that 80 percent of the readers live outside the United States. In 1988, Gannett International published a *Handbook for U.S. Citizens Living Abroad*. Originally produced by ACA, the handbook was updated by *USA Today* in 1988 and sold both in the States and overseas. Topics covered include consular services, voting, customs requirements, passports and visas, driving a car overseas, housing, banking and credit, packing and moving, health preparations, and children's schooling.

Congressional Allies

Support for our endeavors came from an unexpected source in the person of a Democratic representative of the state of Arkansas. Bill Alexander, a long-time friend of Andrew Sundberg, had become an advocate of overseas Americans for their role in successful foreign trade. How did a member of Congress from land-locked Arkansas come to work with U.S. citizens abroad? Rice might be one of the reasons. Arkansas produces 40 percent of the nation's rice, of which it exports 60 percent. As Alexander explained during an interview on Capitol Hill,

> I looked around the House in 1987 and saw that nobody was doing anything about foreign trade. Increasing U.S. exports is the way to trim our bulging foreign trade deficit. To do that U.S. businesspeople need to compete against foreign firms throughout the world. We need to change discriminatory laws and regulations.

Early in 1987 he introduced three bills focusing on Americans abroad. The first one provided for a nonvoting delegate to represent overseas Americans. However, not all overseas Americans supported the legislation. Many were fearful that a special delegate or representative would jeopardize their right to representation by members of Congress from the states where they were last domiciled.

These two points of view have been thoroughly discussed and argued among overseas groups for some years without any weakening of opinions on either side. The second bill, called the Overseas Americans Economic Competition Enhancement Act, provided that American citizens generally would not be subject to U.S. income taxes on income from foreign sources. This measure would bring American tax laws into line with those of other industrialized nations.

The third bill was directed toward American children born overseas. It included provisions that would reduce the residence requirement for the U.S. parent to be able to transmit and automatically grant U.S. citizenship to any child born abroad of a U.S.-citizen parent if that child would otherwise become stateless. It would also allow Americans born overseas to run for the presidency of the United States if they otherwise qualify for that office.

These bills received little support in Congress. Undeterred, Representative Alexander continued to introduce similar bills every year until the 1992 elections. He predicted that Congress would pay attention when it began to address the U.S. trade imbalance and lack of competitiveness with Japan and other nations.

The World Conference

In 1989, chance intervened once more. Representative Mervyn M. Dymally (D-CA), while traveling in Europe, happened to read an article in the *International Herald Tribune* that dealt with the problems of overseas Americans. When he returned to Washington he met with Representative Alexander and Andrew Sundberg of ACA. As a result, Dymally, who chaired the House Foreign Affairs Subcommittee on International Operations, held hearings on November 8, 1989, on the subject of how federal rules and regulations work against Americans living abroad.

Representatives of both Democrats and Republicans Abroad testified. Other witnesses came from Europe representing AARO, FAWCO, ACA, and the American Chambers of Commerce Abroad. Representative Dymally was the first member of Congress who ever held hearings on the whole range of problems faced by overseas residents. It was a breakthrough. After three hours of testimony, Dymally announced that he would set up a bipartisan task force that would go to Paris the following summer to take testimony from Americans at what he called "the scene of the damage."

His decision led to the first World Conference of U.S. Citizens Abroad, held in Paris on July 4-6, 1990, under the sponsorship of the Democratic and Republican Party committees abroad, FAWCO, AARO, ACA, the European Council of American Chambers of Commerce (ECACC), and other American groups.[2]

The congressional delegation was led by Representative Dymally.[3] The federal agencies most concerned with overseas Americans were represented.[4] With over 200 people attending from all over the world, for the first time the European groups met with representatives from the American Business Council of the Gulf Countries. The conference had all of the attributes of a traditional town meeting. Individuals directly affected by discriminatory laws and regulations were able to speak directly to those who make the laws and those who administer them.

Education of American Children Overseas

Among the problem areas discussed at the World Conference was support for the education of American children living overseas. Following are excerpts from testimony by Gail Schoppert, superintendent of the American School in The Hague and president of the board of the European Council of International Schools.

More than 350 schools abroad list themselves as having a U.S. curriculum. Nearly 200 of these are supported in a modest way by the Department of State. These supported schools alone enroll 88,000 pupils in 104 countries. They range from tiny one-teacher schools in places like Shinyang, China, to substantial operations like the American School in Quito with more than 2800 students or Jakarta International School. There are independent schools in such diverse locations as Bucharest, Thessalonika, Moscow, and Cairo. These are not government schools. Most of these institutions were organized by motivated, public-spirited U.S. diplomats and businesspeople in the years after World War II. What are the parents of these students doing abroad? Six thousand five hundred children served by these schools are dependents of U.S. government employees, but the vast majority come from parents involved in American international business.

Most of these independent schools include in their student bodies host country and third-country children. These are leaders of the future in business and diplomacy from more than 100 nations around the world. In an American school they develop positive attitudes toward the United States which will stay with them all of their lives. They are an inexpensive and effective tool for the propagation of democratic ideas and ideals, but the foremost role of the American schools abroad is simple: these institutions provide a fundamental piece of the infrastructure of American business and diplomacy abroad. Without schools for their children, mid-career employees will simply not work in foreign countries. These schools are essential.

Despite their many problems, our American schools abroad have substantial strengths. They send an average of nearly 90 percent of their graduates on to mostly American universities. These schools survive on their own, importing books and supplies and paying for them in U.S. dollars. The combined budgets of the 174 schools which received U.S. State Department suppport last year totaled more than $300 million. Virtually all of these funds are generated by tuitions paid by the parents or organizations which sponsor them.

Because these schools are not governmental agencies they are not normally eligible for the privileges of the diplomatic pouch. Yet the cost of importing books and supplies can be prohibitive.

In the past the schools and directors and teachers have enjoyed the full backing of diplomatic posts. This had included shipping and clearance of goods, duty-free privileges, access to the diplomatic pouch, the use of embassy health facilities, commissary privileges, and preferences in obtaining surplus American furniture and supplies. Almost all of these support services are being cut!

Ken Vogel, director of the international school in Ouagadougou in Burkina Faso, wrote to the conference organizers as follows:

> The school has been denied access to the embassy package-pouch. For example, we were told in January we could no longer use the pouch for our supplies. We then had to order them from the U.S. via air freight. We ordered $3,500 worth of supplies. The air freight charges brought the total up to $10,000, then the local government charged us $10,000 worth of duty on the goods. Thus we had to pay over $20,000 for goods which normally would have cost us $3,500.

Another sore point: Libraries on U.S. military bases are open only to Department of Defense schools. They should be accessible to all U.S. schools in the area. Kevin Hale, a father of three in South Korea, made this point:

> While thousands of Korean nationals go on base everyday for everything from playing golf on the military golf course to cleaning military toilets, U.S. citizens are usually denied access. These thousands of Korean employees of the base can use the base library and they do—there is a large Korean language section—while U.S. citizens are denied the same privilege. I am happy to share our library with Koreans or anyone else, but it is infuriating to be locked out of the very library that is built with your own taxes. It is hard to understand how the security of the U.S. will be threatened by elementary and junior high school kids using the library.

Dr. Schoppert requested that all American schools receiving State Department recognition be given the use of

Army Post Office (APO) and diplomatic pouch facilities and that the definition of schools eligible for State Department support be broadened as far as possible. At the very least, these suggestions should be implemented in areas designated as hardship posts by the State Department. He added:

> The attitude of the United States government toward the education of overseas American children is in striking contrast to that of our major trading competitors. Japan, Germany, and France spend millions of dollars each year to provide educational materials, facilities, and teachers for their private sector children. Not only does the U.S. govenment spend little for our children, Uncle Sam taxes the education allowances given to American parents who live abroad.

Taxation as a Trade Issue

George Baccash, a resident of Saudi Arabia representing the American Business Council of the Gulf Countries, offered the following testimony on taxation of Americans resident overseas:

> U.S. tax on Americans abroad is an issue that we need to address, because it is a barrier among many other barriers that we have, whether corporate or individual income taxes, Social Security benefits, citizenship, voting rights, or education. These barriers reduce our ability to conduct business in the global marketplace and therefore contribute directly to America's trade and budget deficits, which in themselves are additional burdens on the American economy. Tax is the concern, but trade is the issue.
>
> We have to avoid the perception back home that if you live overseas you are a fat cat in the lap of luxury and you don't pay your fair share of taxes. We know that is wrong. Tax incentives, such as the exclusion for foreign source earned income, assist in expanding exports by enabling U.S. corporations to place American citizens abroad. Every American abroad is an export salesperson. By requesting American made goods and services Americans abroad are the salespeople

for American business whether it is for the company they work for or by purchasing American made products for their own consumption.

Let me illustrate this with an example from Saudi Arabia. For whatever reason the United Kingdom sold a tremendous amount of military hardware to the Saudis. There has been an influx of 5,000 to 6,000 British citizens in the past year. Tremendous changes are taking place in the supermarkets. You can't go down and buy Eggo waffles because they have been replaced with scones. On our compound GM products are going away and you are seeing more and more Land Rovers and Jaguars. In this regard somebody in the States has lost jobs or jobs aren't expanding. Depending on whose statistics you believe, one American abroad generates from two to eleven jobs in the United States. Therefore expatriates generate exports, which generate U.S. jobs and domestic tax revenues. Simply stated, tax revenues will increase and deficits will be reduced.

Citizenship

Kathleen de Carbuccia explained the restrictions placed on the transmission of U.S. citizenship to children born abroad of American parents as well as those adopted by American citizens. She presented several case histories, including these:

Ben Davis is an American and a Harvard trained lawyer working at the International Chamber of Commerce in Paris, the leading institution for international arbitration in the world. Ben and his American wife have two adopted children in France: Anne-Laure, born in 1988, and Daniel, born in 1990. Despite living in France, he and his wife are raising their children in an American family setting. They want them to be American citizens. Under current law, however, the only way he can do this is to quit his job, move back to the U.S. and reside there permanently.

Caroline Van Herpen: I was born an overseas American in Switzerland. My mother is American and my father French. Today I am living with my Dutch husband and my son Max, born in 1989, who is an American, and my daugher Julia, born in 1986, who is not. How did we become a divided family? To go back a long time, I spoke English at home as a child. At fourteen I left home to attend boarding school in Maryland. It was not just any school, but the one that had educated all of the women in my American family for several generations. After three years I went back to Europe and graduated from the American College in Paris in 1971 and continued on to the L'Institut d'Études Politiques in Paris. In 1974, I was twenty-two and went to Washington, D.C., because my ambition was to work in Congress. I was an intern in the House Republican Conference. I took a master's in international affairs at Johns Hopkins. At graduation I was hired by large American corporation to audit their overseas operations. At Johns Manville they needed someone who spoke several languages, someone with experience traveling and living abroad, and those Americans are in short supply in the U.S. I know from hiring auditors myself.

From 1978 to 1984 I worked for Manville all over the world, traveling for the better part of each year making sure that American corporate assets were safe and well managed. By 1983 I had more work at headquarters so I bought a house in Denver, hoping to settle down.

Then the company decided to transfer my Dutch citizen fiancé to Paris. In 1985 I married him and in May 1986 our daughter was born in Paris. At that time, the law required that I, the American parent, be able to show that I had spent at least ten years on American soil prior to her birth. When I counted up all of the time I had worked and studied in America, it only added up to eight years and a few months. My daughter could not be an American at birth. If I had been at my desk in the Denver headquarters instead of traveling at a grueling pace for an American business, I would have had more than ten years in the U.S.

It is quite distressing that my services to an American company caused me not to fulfill an obscure requirement in the law and as a result my daughter is not a U.S. citizen. Five months after she was born, Congress passed an amendment of the law reducing the requirement to five years. I qualified under the new law, but since the law did not extend to any child already born, Julia still could not be an American. My son Max, born in 1989, is American. At present Julia travels on an indefinite visa so that we can all go to America together as we have done twice. There the immigration officer

asks me to explain why Julia doesn't have an American passport, but it is not easy to explain and even more difficult to
accept. Meanwhile this law does not alter the way we feel or
the way we raise our children.

My husband may be Dutch, but American culture is part of
our everyday life. At age seventeen my husband spent a year
as an exchange student in Michigan. He loved America and
came back for graduate school on a fellowship. He's worked
thirteen years for the same American company. We speak
English at home as I did as a child. Julia's mother tongue is
English and she is learning French as well and she will later
learn other languages. Naturally my children won't be American in the same way as they would have been if we had stayed
in Denver, but it doesn't make them any less worthy or less
useful to their country.

The current law is not only unjust but out of step with our
times. In a world of increasing interdependence, the United
States should treasure each and every one of its overseas citizens. Acknowledging them only as taxpayers is an insult and
a mistake. The overwhelming majority of Americans abroad
care very strongly about the United States and at the very
least American children born overseas grow to harbor
benevolent feelings towards America and act accordingly
wherever we live and whatever we do. No country in this
day and age can afford to dismiss such a mine of international goodwill.

In concluding the meeting, Representative Dymally
called for the creation of an intergency task force in Washington composed of representatives from the U.S. Departments of State, Justice, Treasury, Commerce, and Health
and Human Services to address the problems of overseas
citizens. He announced tentative plans for congressional
hearings in October 1990. However, the military crisis in
the Gulf and Kuwait intervened and the proposed hearings were indefinitely postponed. The task force did not
materialize.

The World Federation of Americans Abroad

Fortunately, the enthusiasm generated by the conference was strong and the six sponsoring groups began to plan for a permanent umbrella organization. The conference copresidents, Stephanie Simonard and John F. Crawford, president of the ECACC, proceeded with the establishment of the World Federation of Americans Abroad (WFAA). The task proved to be difficult. Although the groups agreed on the need for such an organization, they did not agree on whether it would be only an umbrella organization or a broader-based membership organization. As a coalition, WFAA shied away from accepting individual membership, reasoning that drawing a member from a sponsoring organization would weaken the sponsor. Less than a year later, the two political party organizations represented by Jim Fees (Republican) and Peter Alegi (Democrat) pulled out of WFAA and formed the Federated League of Americans Abroad (FLAAG).

The remaining groups—ACA, FAWCO, AARO, and ECACC—remained committed and welcomed the addition of the American Business Council of the Gulf Countries, which counts among its members 700 American firms representing 45,000 U.S. citizens. Shortly thereafter WFAA was incorporated in the State of Delaware and received the sponsorship of AT&T, thus enabling the organization to undertake further efforts in Washington.

Notes

1.   Austria, Belgium, Canada, Finland, France, Greece, Germany, Ireland, Italy, Luxembourg, the Netherlands, Norway, Portugal, Spain, Sweden, Switzerland, and the United Kingdom.
2.   The United States Chamber of Commerce in Washington, D.C.; the Asian-Pacific Council of American Chambers of Commerce (Taipei); the Association of American Chambers of Commerce in Latin America (Mexico City); the American Association of Singapore; the Retired Officers Association (Kaiserslautern);

the Benjamin Franklin Post of the Veterans of Foreign Wars (Paris); the Association of American Wives of Europeans (Paris); the American Clubs of Brussels, Paris, and Lyon. Together these groups represent an estimated total of 151,090 individuals.

3. Representatives Ted Weiss (D-NY), George W. Crockett, Jr. (D-MI), William Frenzel (R-MN), Jaime B. Fuster (PR), Ben Blaz (GU), Paul E. Gilmor, (R-OH), Donald M. Payne (D-N), Donald E. Lukens (R-OH) and Barbara Vucanovich (R-NY).

4. Internal Revenue Service—Donald Bergherm, assistant commissioner (international); Department of State—Elizabeth Tamposi, assistant secretary for consular affairs; Carmen DiPlacido and Ann Swift, oveseas citizens services; Federal Voting Assistance Program—Henry Valentino, director; Social Security Administration—Barbara Wilson, federal benefits officer (Rome).

10

Some Constructive Conferences (1991–1993)

ALTHOUGH the World Federation was still lobbying on a shoestring, with the help of AT&T it could now turn to a professional who could prepare the second World Conference of U.S. Citizens Abroad, planned for June 1991 in Washington. David Hamod, a consultant, set up a series of informal meetings, which he called "doorknocks," with members of Congress and staff members of congressional committees. He divided the Federation delegates into teams and then scheduled appointments, matching the issues with appropriate congressional committees. When Representative Dymally stepped down from the chairmanship of the International Operations Subcommittee we lost a good friend and supporter, but fortunately we found a new one in Representative Howard L. Berman (D-CA), who succeeded him as chair of that subcommittee.

A WFAA pilot program was presented that would develop more active and flexible export-promotion strategies. A postconference report cited some of the testimony before the subcommittee.

All of the important issues were raised during the two days of meetings. Henry Valentino, director of the Federal Voting Assistance Program, promised to seek technical amendments to the Uniformed and Overseas Citizens

Absentee Voting Act to allow the electronic transmission of absentee ballots.

Measures for the security for overseas citizens, particularly in the Middle East in Iran, Lebanon, and the Gulf nations, were called for by Howard Campbell, a resident of Saudi Arabia during the Gulf War.

Kathleen de Carbuccia and Michael Adler, who were heading up the WFAA Citizenship Committee, set out to convince Congress to modify three remaining areas in the law that overseas Americans found it difficult or impossible to comply with. First, they sought to reduce the transmission requirement for children born overseas of one American parent from five to only one or two years. Second, they sought to modify an expeditious naturalization procedure that already existed under section 322 of the law to enable U.S. citizens living abroad to have their adopted children become Americans and, at the same time, to provide "fallback" protection to other children who might not benefit under the first reform. It gave all U.S. parents (including adoptive parents) the right to apply to the Immigration and Naturalization Service (INS) for certificates of citizenship for children under eighteen, but only when they were in the United States and intended to live there. But this authority was of no real use to Americans who were earning their living by working abroad. Adler and de Carbuccia proposed to remove the "intent to reside permanently" requirement from the section.

A third matter was the reinstatement of those who had had their citizenship taken from them for failure to reside in the United States when they were teenagers and young adults. This issue concerned approximately 5,000 individuals born between 1934 and 1952. The citizenship committee felt that those individuals should be given a chance to be reinstated as citizens if they so desired. I once again began to hope that this effort would restore American citizenship to my own children.

These three points had been raised by both Adler and de Carbuccia, as well as by representatives of other American groups, at the hearings of the International Operations

Subcommittee in Washington in 1989 and at the first World Conference in Paris in 1990. Kathleen de Carbuccia raised them again before the International Operations Subcommittee of the House Foreign Affairs Committee, chaired by Representative Berman, who was sympathetic to the cause of Americans abroad. The legislative staff member in charge of this matter for Representative Berman was Beth Hilliard. Michael Adler remembers her first meeting with Hilliard vividly: "She listened attentively, understood what we needed, and she took on our cause as her own. It was wonderful to finally be 'heard.'"

On the Republican side, Adler met another key staff member, Carmel Fisk, minority counsel to the Immigration Subcommittee, who worked for Representative Bill McCollum of Florida. Fisk, like Hilliard, was bright, competent, understanding, and willing to help, and they understood that living abroad didn't make one a second-class citizen. This was a refreshing departure from the reception we had often received from congressional staff—some of whom actually asked us why, if we felt so strongly about having U.S. citizenship for our children, we didn't simply move back to the United States. At the same time, even with the cooperation of Hilliard and Fisk and continual input from Eugene Pugliese, majority counsel to the Mazzoli subcommittee, it would be three more years before Congress would act on our concerns.

Addressing the Local-Hire Policy

Also at that meeting, the particularly sensitive issue of the exclusion of U.S. overseas residents from local-hire positions in consulates and embassies was brought to the attention of Senator John D. Rockefeller IV (D-WV), who introduced an amendment to a State Department authorization bill making U.S. citizens eligible to be hired for Foreign Service National (FSN) jobs. At that time, the United States was the only country in the world that would not hire its own citizens in overseas federal government posts.

In his introductory speech on the Senate floor, Senator Rockefeller stated,

> I am not talking about high-security jobs or jobs where a national from a host country is needed. I am talking about the hundreds of administrative jobs, from drivers to librarians to secretaries to accountants, now occupied by other employees, that might easily be filled by American citizens.
>
> It is deplorable that the U.S. government discriminates against potential employees on the basis of nationality. But the fact that it discriminates only against American citizens is simply ridiculous. My amendment will not require the embassy to end its preferencial hiring program for embassy dependents and spouses. It will not force embassies to hire Americans who have not passed security clearances. What it will do is permit the State Department to hire U.S. citizens if it so desires.

It is difficult to trace the reasons for this policy. It was clearly spelled out, however, in the Foreign Service Act of 1980, which allowed for the hiring of only two categories of people abroad: foreign national employees and U.S. citizens who are family members of government employees. The State Department had always interpreted that provision as precluding the employment of other American citizens.

Action to change the situation was spearheaded by Denise Liebowitz, an American woman living in Belgium. Leibowitz was married to a Foreign Service officer and had become interested in this issue in the 1970s when her husband was posted to Brussels for the third time. She made inquiries at the embassy personnel office. Although she had been with her husband on previous assignments to Brussels, spoke good French, and knew the work and jobs at the embassy, she was told that no Americans need apply. Dependents were hired for low-paying clerical jobs, but professional positions were not open to spouses of Foreign Service officers. They went to foreign citizens. When Liebowitz joined the American Women's Club of Brussels, she learned about FAWCO. She had found a platform, and that led her into action with WFAA.

American citizens abroad recognize that many FSN positions require continuity, competence in the host country language, and knowledge of local institutions, laws, and customs. But many U.S. citizens who are long-term host country residents do in fact possess these qualifications. Many of the FSN jobs are held by third-country nationals, evidence that these jobs do not necessarily have to be staffed with host country nationals and that qualified Americans should be eligible to compete for them. The FSN employees are compensated with American taxpayer dollars, yet American taxpayers were, by law, automatically excluded from these positions.

A case brought to the attention of Leibowitz was that of a professional translator who had applied for a position with the embassy in Tel Aviv and received a curt reply that his application could not be considered because he was an American citizen. He wrote,

Aside from the absurdity of the reply—who can translate better into the American idiom than a native-born American?—I wonder what American citizenship is worth if the very government that granted it views it as a liability?

At the conclusion of the meeting, Kathleen de Carbuccia, newly elected cochair, declared that the second World Conference marked a watershed for the World Federation: "We learned some valuable lessons about communicating our concerns to Washington and will build on those lessons in the future."

Benjamin Gilman (R-NY), a key member of the House Foreign Affairs Committee, concurred. He told the delegation that they had taken their first step toward putting Americans overseas on the political map.

Addressing Health Insurance

After the successful conference in Washington, a meeting in Walldorf, Germany, was organized for April 1992 around the theme of health care for veterans and other retirees. More than 200 people attended the one-day seminar held near the U.S. Army base. The health care insurance coverage problems due to the CHAMPUS cutoff at age sixty-five for veterans and the lack of Medicare for both veteran retirees and others were the major complaints by attendees. American insurance companies are reluctant to sell insurance to people living outside the United States, and European firms do not want to take on people who are over sixty-two. Speakers at the conference, including Major General Michael Scotti, Commanding General of the Seventh Medical Command headquarters in Heidelberg, were not optimistic about congressional action. However, a need had been clearly demonstrated, and we determined to bring up the issue at the second Washington conference of the Federation, to be held on June 24-25, 1992.

Our meetings were once again planned by David Hamod, who divided the delegates into teams as before and set up appointments with administration officials and key members of Congress and their staffs. Discussions on the whole range of problems experienced by overseas citizens were scheduled. Probably owing to our status as World War II veterans, Andrew Sundberg and I drew the CHAMPUS and Medicare issues and talked with staff members of the Senate Appropriations Subcommittee on Defense, who were sympathetic, but the final answer—although not expressed in those terms—was that if retirees want Medicare let them come back to the United States to live.

Citizenship Issues

Citizenship still ranked high on the list of areas to be discussed. In January 1992 Representative Bill Alexander introduced a bill that called for a reduction of the five-year transmission requirement to one year. Representative Mazzoli, chairman of the House subcommittee, grouped this with other proposals and held hearings on them in

May 1992. Adler, who had traveled from Paris to testify for WFAA, did her best to convince the subcommittee members to reduce the five-year requirement. They were just as determined to resist what they thought was a kind of automatic citizenship conferred on children whom they considered as being too far removed from American life. During these 1992 doorknock meetings Adler and de Carbuccia were still unable to convince the House subcommittee to ease the transmission requirement. They were, however, able to make headway on the proposals for expeditious naturalization procedures for children born abroad (although the subcommittee insisted on limiting this procedure to children with an American parent or grandparent who had resided for at least five years in the United States) and for the reinstatement of the 5,000 former Americans who had been stripped of their citizenship for failure to fulfill the residence period stipulated under previous law. We were acutely aware that these solutions, although they would help most children of Americans abroad, would not solve the citizenship problems of all overseas Americans—many families who really cared about U.S. citizenship would be left out. We also realized that the naturalization procedure proposed by the Subcommittee would be cumbersome for families abroad. Nonetheless, we reasoned, it was preferable to accept the possible rather than insist on perfection and come up empty-handed in the end.

The following months, when the revised bill was sent to the full Committee on the Judiciary, "our" two proposals were included! Adler was ecstatic. When the bill was passed by the full House of Representatives in the fall of 1992, we hoped that it would finally be enacted into law. Unfortunately, owing to the press of congressional business, the 102nd Congress adjourned with no action by the Senate.

Since all legislation that is not enacted "dies" at the end of each Congress, a new bill, H.R.-783, was introduced by Representative Mazzoli in January 1993. Mazzoli called for further hearings in March 1993, and Adler was again invited to testify. This time she did not have to make the trip from Paris because she was living in Charlottesville, Virginia, where her French husband was taking six months of his sabbatical year to teach at the University of Virginia. She closed her testimony with this statement:

> May I respectfully remind the Subcommittee on International Law, Immigration and Refugees that the citizenship problems experienced by Americans overseas do not involve international law and that we and our children are neither immigrants nor refugees. We are Americans like everyone here. No better for sure, but certainly no worse. We'd like to be treated fairly and not be penalized merely because we live abroad.

About this time Americans abroad happily found an ally in the newly appointed Ambassador to France, Pamela Harriman. At an AAWE luncheon in October 1993, Harriman acknowledged the unofficial ambassadorial role of American women living in foreign countries. She also understood immediately the importance of H.R.-783 and offered her help.

H.R.-783 passed the House and the Senate in two different versions in November 1993 during the last hours of the first congressional session. It was not until a year later—on October 24, 1994—that it finally became law.

Summing up, Michael Adler said,

> I think we pushed Congress as far as it was willing to go on citizenship at this time. To get everything we want for our children, Americans abroad will have to do a better job convincing Americans at home that we are not second class citizens simply because we do not live within the borders of the United States.

Summing Up

ON JUNE 22–24, 1993, the World Federation of Americans Abroad (WFAA) held its last doorknock conference in Washington. In addition to energizing efforts already in motion on voting rights, citizenship, and education, new ground was broken in at least two important areas: American commercial interests overseas and embassy and consulate closures.

With Americans expressing so much concern about the need for economic growth, the issue of "business competitiveness" was highlighted by WFAA delegation members. Americans abroad play a key role in generating U.S.-based jobs. Preliminary data using private sector estimates and Commerce Department figures ($1 billion in exports equals 22,800 direct jobs) indicate that exports generated by Americans abroad ($448 billion) were directly or indirectly responsible for nearly 18 million jobs in the United States in 1992. WFAA urged support for a bill sponsored by Representative Bill Archer (R-TX), which would create jobs for American workers and help to place U.S. companies on a level playing field with their international competitors.

In a related letter to State Department officials, WFAA leadership highlighted why increased cooperation with Americans abroad has become more important than ever.

As the State Department seeks to develop a stronger role in promoting U.S. economic interests overseas, the department's natural allies are the 3 million Americans abroad. They can share expertise and contacts gained from decades of working in foreign markets. Americans overseas—as "unofficial ambassadors" for the United States—are our country's best salespeople, creating a demand for American goods and increasing our nation's exposure internationally. It has become conventional wisdom that in the near future even larger numbers of Americans are needed abroad to defend U.S. market share, maintain domestic jobs, and enhance U.S. exports.

Because of the State Department's decision to shut down fourteen embassies and consulates in 1993, WFAA delegates urged State Department officials to study financial self-sufficiency for U.S. consulates throughout the world.[1]

In concluding this last doorknock, the WFAA delegation gave awards to two members of Congress: Senator John D. Rockefeller III for his efforts to open up local-hire jobs in U.S. embassies and consulates to Americans resident in the host countries, and Representative Howard L. Berman, who played an instrumental role in promoting WFAA-generated citizenship provisions. A third award went to *USA Today* for its outstanding coverage of overseas Americans.

Since the very successful series of meetings in Washingon and despite the conclusion of AT&T sponsorship, WFAA has maintained its contacts and channels in Washington, continuing its role as spokesman for overseas Americans.

Embassy Employment

The Rockefeller amendment had passed in 1991, but establishing pay scales proved to be complicated. In April 1994 President Clinton signed new legislation, again sponsored by Senator Rockefeller, giving American local-hire employees pay and benefit equity with their foreign national counterparts. Finally, in 1995 the Office of Foreign

Service National Personnel was given a new name: the Office of Overseas Employment. According to an article in the July 1995 issue of *STATE*,

The establishment of this office also recognizes the expanding role of and our increasing reliance on Foreign Service Nationals [FSNs], as well as family members and other U.S. citizens.[2]

Positions hitherto reserved for FSNs in political, economic, consular, and administrative functions as well as public diplomacy are now open to U.S. citizen overseas residents. The way has been cleared of all obstacles that hindered individuals applying for available jobs.

Medicare and CHAMPUS

In 1993, at the last doorknock meeting in Washington, the Health Financing Office of the Department of Defense (DOD) made it clear that because of financial considerations the decision to extend CHAMPUS benefits beyond age sixty-five would have to come from Congress. Congress had its own budget constraints and the Federation delegation did not hold out much hope for congressional action. They have been proved right.

As for Medicare, the latest information dates from November 1993, when Ambassador to France Pamela Harriman relayed Washington's answer to a WFAA question as to whether Americans resident overseas would benefit from the Clinton health care plan. The answer was no.

Education of American Children Overseas

Dr. Gail Schoppert, who now directs the American School of Warsaw, Poland, had received assurances at the 1991 doorknock that surplus materials from DOD schools in

Germany could be donated to State Department-sponsored schools in Eastern Europe. The transfer began quickly. Last year Dr. Schoppert received three truckloads of excess furniture from DOD base schools that are closing down. Washington officials also agreed to a further request that U.S. commissary privileges be extended to teachers in hardship posts. Schoppert has reported that American teachers in Warsaw now have access to the embassy commissary, greatly facilitating their life "in a city where standing in a variety of lines may take hours they could otherwise devote to…correcting papers."

The American school in Warsaw is one of the many rapidly growing American schools in Eastern Europe where American businesspeople have come to work and brought their families.

Business Competitiveness

At this writing, a private group of American businesspeople is conducting a survey of American firms that employ Americans in their overseas subsidiaries. The survey covers the hiring of U.S. citizens versus foreign citizens, where and how many employees are stationed abroad, and how overseas operations contribute to overall revenues. The conclusions of this survey will help make overseas Americans visible to policymakers in Washington, showing them how citizens abroad create jobs and business in both international and domestic sectors.

Absentee Voting

The Federal Voting Assistance Program administers the Uniformed and Overseas Citizens Absentee Voting Act, which covers the needs of members of the armed forces, their spouses and dependents, and overseas citizens—approximately 6 million Americans. Procedures for voting have become more and more simplified. Thirty-eight states now allow faxing of some of the steps to registration. A toll-free number is available to call from fifty foreign countries to obtain information. A new guide to voting was published in December 1995. Although not all of the states have unified procedures for registration and balloting, organizations of overseas citizens continue to monitor the system. Notarization of ballots, still required by seven states, is a real impediment, particularly with the large numbers of consulate closings. Some Americans are obliged to travel long distances to reach a U.S. consulate.

Citizenship

Parents of children of born and residing abroad now have an additional way to obtain U.S. citizenship for their minor children under PL 103-416. The Immigration and Naturalization Service will administer the new law. Although there has been some delay in the first year of this new authority's existence, this expeditious naturalization process will no doubt be fully operational shortly. While this new law is far from ideal, it permits most of the children and grandchildren of Americans abroad who were previously excluded to become citizens.

In addition, the group of former U.S. citizens born between 1934 and 1952, who had lost their U.S. citizenship as teenagers and young adults, can now be reinstated as U.S. citizens through a simple swearing-in process before a U.S. consular officer.

On the whole, everyone who has been associated with these efforts in whatever capacity in the past thirty-five years can be pleased with what has been achieved. Nothing would have been accomplished without them and the organizations they supported. In one form or another, all of the issues have been brought to the attention of the three branches of the federal government. Some were never fully considered by any agency; others were at least partially corrected; and in a few cases there has been complete success.

We have come to see that passing a new law is only the first step of a much larger process. Implementation can present further barriers.

A more realistic view of overseas citizens has been gained by a few members of Congress who have become our friends. The difficulty is that members of Congress come and go. After Election Day we are obliged to start all over again with newly elected representatives and senators who may not recognize the significance of the issues facing overseas Americans. We must find ways to demonstrate that residence in a foreign country and the acquisition of another language abroad does not make a person an integral part of a foreign culture, nor does he or she become any less American. Instead, overseas Americans become more mindful of the world and more valuable to the future of their homeland, the United States.

Notes

1.   The new American Center of Geneva has been created and opened through the joint efforts of local American residents and the State Department. It offers consular, commerical, and cultural services for the people of Switzerland.

2.   Formerly the *Department of State Newsletter.*

Epilogue

In MAY 1995 my children, Robert Michaux and Carolyn Michaux Granier-Deferre, were reinstated as American citizens at the American consulate in Paris under section 324 of P.L. 103-416. Their minor children are eligible for expeditious naturalization under section 322 of the same law. In December 1995 my granddaughter, Karine Granier-Deferre, a French citizen, graduated from the University of Missouri with degrees in international affairs and journalism. As a member of the new Euro-American generation, and with an equal command of French and English, she will most likely pursue an international career.

WFAA delegates with Senator John D. Rockefeller IV, June 1993. From left: Barbara Johnson, Eugene Abrams, Norma Lehmann-Vogelweid, Gary Eubank, Helen Tange, Michael Adler, Senator Rockefeller, Denise Liebowitz, Alan Conkey, Roberta Enschede, Kathleen de Carbuccia.

APPENDIX A

ORGANIZATIONS OF AMERICANS RESIDENT OVERSEAS

American Aid Society. A private, nonprofit, volunteer organization founded in 1922. Although the American Embassy provides office space for the Society, donations are its sole source of financial assistance for Americans in temporary difficulty in France. A limited number of grants for elderly, disabled, or sick Americans residing in France are also funded through gifts. C/o U.S. Consulate, 2 rue Saint Florentin, 75008 Paris, France.

American Business Council of the Gulf Countries. An affiliate of the U.S. Chamber of Commerce representing 700 U.S. companies doing business in the Persian Gulf region. P.O. Box 9281, World Trade Center, Dubai, U.A.E.

American Chamber of Commerce in France. A nonprofit organization founded in 1894 that promotes French-American trade and economic relations, with affiliates in several French cities. Activities for its American and French members include conferences, seminars, and business services. Publications include a quarterly magazine and a membership directory that contains a list of American businesses in France. 21 Avenue George V, 75008 Paris, France.

American Citizens Abroad. A nonprofit, nonpartisan public service organization founded in 1978 that acts on issues facing U.S. citizens overseas such as citizenship, taxation, representation, and health care. Offers a full range of health insurance and annuities. Publications include news reports and press releases. Members in more than ninety countries; country contacts on six continents on e-mail and Internet. P.O. Box 321, 1211 Geneva, 12, Switzerland.

American Hospital of Paris. Founded in 1910, this 187-bed health care facility offers a full range of diagnostic and treatment services, including an emergency room open 24 hours a day. It is a private, not-for-profit institution recognized by the American Joint Commission on Accreditation of Healthcare Organizations. 63 Bd. Victor Hugo, 92202 Neuilly-sur-Seine, France.

American Legion, Paris Post I. The first American Legion post was founded in Paris in 1919 by veterans of World War I.

American Women's Group in Paris. Founded in 1931. Activities include monthly luncheon meetings, guided tours, some educational courses, and fund-raising activities in order to award scholarships to French students for study in the United States. 22 bis rue Petrarque, 75116 Paris, France.

American Overseas Memorial Day Association. Founded in 1920, this association plans, carries out, and pays for ceremonies on Memorial Day at U.S. military cemeteries in Europe. It also arranges for the placing of American flags on the graves of American veterans buried in local cemeteries in Europe. All activities are funded by the members. 34 Avenue de New York, 75016 Paris, France.

Association of American Residents Overseas. Founded in 1973, this nonpartisan nonprofit organization is dedicated to protecting the basic civil rights of Americans resident overseas. With members living in more than twenty countries, AARO concentrates on issues such as absentee voting, citizenship, taxation, and certain social benefits, including Medicare. A group health plan is available to members. Quarterly newsletter, topical seminars, meetings. B.P. 127, 92154 Suresnes Cedex, France.

Association of American Wives of Europeans. Founded in 1961 with the primary goal of protecting the U.S. citizenship rights of its members and their children. Professional and social networking, cultural events, special-interest seminars, celebration of American holidays. Activities are directed toward teaching American traditions, language, and culture to the children of members. Publications include a monthly newsletter. B.P. 127, 92154 Suresnes Cedex, France.

American Dual National Citizenship Committee. An informal organization established in 1970 as the financing vehicle for the AAWE Supreme Court brief in the _Bellei_ case.

Bipartisan Committee for Absentee Voting. Founded in Paris in 1965 by Alfred E. Davidson, then chairman of the Democratic Party Committee—Europe, and Harvey S. Gerry, then chairman of the Republican Party Committee—Europe, this committee began working with Congress to set up a federal registration procedure to replace archaic state registration procedures for absentee balloting. Ten years later, these efforts culminated in the Overseas Voting Rights Act of 1975.

Bipartisan Committee for Medicare Overseas. Founded in Paris in 1967 by Alfred E. Davidson and Harvey S. Gerry (see above) with the objective of persuading Congress to extend Medicare benefits to overseas residents. This legislative effort was successful in the Senate but was finally defeated in the House of Representatives.

Council of Americans Resident Abroad. Organized around 1950 in Mexico City by Carl D.Ross, copublisher of an English-language newspaper. In a 1955 brochure it deplored the disenfranchisement of Americans abroad, their exclusion from certain Social Security programs, taxation without representation, and complex rules on citizenship.

Democrats Abroad (France). Represents the Democratic Party in France. Encourages and enables Americans resident in France to participate in the political process and to vote in all national elections. 5 rue Bargue, 75015 Paris, France.

European Council of American Chambers of Commerce. An umbrella organization founded in 1965 that coordinates the activities of the twenty-two member American Chambers of Commerce in Europe and the Mediterrean area. These chambers, members of the U.S. Chamber of Commerce in Washington, D.C., have a combined corporate membership of more than 18,000 firms. Their mission is to promote commercial, financial, and industrial relations between the United States and the various countries of Europe. C/o William H. Edgar, 5309 Burling Terrace, Bethesda, MD 20814.

English-Language Library for the Blind. Established in 1980. Offers works of English and American literature recorded on standard cassettes to blind and partially sighted persons in France and twenty other countries. Volunteers carry out the work of recording, cassette copying, and selecting and mailing books. 35 rue Lemercier, 75017 Paris, France.

Federation of American Women's Clubs Overseas. Founded in 1931 in London. The seven original clubs have grown to sixty-two, with a total membership of 15,000 in thirty-one countries overseas. As early as 1953, FAWCO began to work actively for absentee voting rights for

Americans overseas. Serves as a support network for American women residing abroad and is a major force in promoting international understanding. Main address: C/o Rebecca Tan, President, Frohmestrasse 73, Haus 22, D-22459, Hamburg, Germany. Publications available through the FAWCO Resource Center, c/o American Women's Club of The Hague, Nieuwe Duinweg 25, 2587AB Den Haag, Netherlands.

Federation of International American Clubs. In 1978 this group joined with FAWCO to establish the short-lived Council of Americans Resident Overseas (CARO) based in Ireland.

League of Americans Resident Abroad. Founded in Paris in 1965 by William W. Brinkerhoff and James J. Wadsworth, a former representative to the United Nations; dedicated to the protection of the civil rights of overseas residents. It developed an insurance program but never recruited enough members and was dissolved before 1970.

Republicans Abroad (France). Represents the Republican Party in France. Encourages and enables Americans resident in France to exercise their rights in the political process and to participate in the activities of the Republican Party. C/o Phyllis Morgan, Chair, chez Madame Habourdin, 87 Av. Mozart, 75016 Paris, France.

Veterans of Foreign Wars, Benjamin Franklin Post 605. Founded in 1920. Organizes and participates in veteran-related ceremonies such as the rekindling of the Flame of the Unknown Soldier at the Arc de Triomphe on Benjamin Franklin's birthday, January 16, and the American Memorial Day ceremony at Belleau Wood. C/o John Davis, 7 rue Agar, 75016 Paris, France.

World Federation of Americans Abroad. A nonprofit, nonpartisan federation of American organizations dedicated to representing the 3 million Americans who live and work overseas. Through lobbying efforts it seeks to improve U.S. laws and policies in the areas of citizenship, taxation, voting, access to earned medical and Social Security benefits, business competitiveness, and general U.S. policy toward overseas residents. Founding members: AARO, FAWCO, ACA, ECACC. B.P. 127, 92154 Suresnes, Cedex, France.

APPENDIX B

Following are sections of the Immigration and Nationality Act as written before and after amendments cited in *The Unknown Ambassadors*. In all cases involving citizenship the reader is referred to the Act itself, which is available from the Government Printing Office, and advised to seek legal advice.

TITLE III—NATIONALITY AND NATURALIZATION (May 1, 1995)

Chapter I—Nationality at Birth and by Collective Naturalization

Nationals and Citizens of the United States at Birth

Sec. 301 The following shall be nationals and citizens of the United States at birth:

(a) a person born in the United States, and subject to the jurisdiction thereof;

(c) a person born outside of the United States, and its outlying possessions of parents both of whom are citizens of the United States and one of whom has had a residence in the United States or one of its outlying possessions; prior to the birth of such person;

(g) a person born outside of the geographical limits of the United States and its outlying possessions of parents one of whom is an alien, and the other a citizen of the United States, who, prior to the birth of such person, was physically present in the United States or its outlying possessions for a period or periods totaling not less than five years, at least two of which were after attaining the age of fourteen years: Provided, That any periods of honorable service in the Armed Forces of the United States, or periods of employment with the United States Government or with an international organization as that term is defined in section 1 of the International Organization Immunities Act (59 Stat. 669; 22 U.S.C. 288) by such citizen parent, or any periods during which such citizen parent is physically present abroad as the dependent unmarried son or daughter and a member of the household of a person (A) honorably serving with the Armed Forces of the United States, or (B) employed by the United States Government or an international organization as defined in section 1 of the International Organizations Immunities Act, may be included in order to satisfy the physical-presence requirement of this paragraph. This proviso shall be applicable to persons born on or after December 24, 1952, to the same extent as if it had become effective in its present form on that date.

Chapter 2—Nationality through Naturalization

Child Born Outside the United States; Application for Certificate of Citizenship Requirements.

Sec. 322. (a) A parent who is a citizen of the United States may apply to the Attorney General for a certificate of citizenship on behalf of a child born outside the United States. The Attorney General shall issue such a certificate of citizenship upon proof to the satisfaction of the Attorney General that the following conditions have been fulfilled:

(1) At least one parent is a citizen of the United States, whether by birth or naturalization.

(2) The child is physically present in the United States pursuant to a lawful admission.

(3) The child is under 18 and in the legal custody of the citizen parent.

(4) If the citizen parent is an adoptive parent of the child, the child was adopted by the citizen parent before the child reached the age of 16 years and the child meets the requirement for being a child under subparagraph (E) or (F) of section 101(b)(1).

(5) If the citizen parent has not been physically present in the United States or its outlying possessions for a period or periods totaling not less than five years, at least two of which were after attaining the age of fourteen years—

(A) the child is residing permanently in the United States with the citizen parent, pursuant to a lawful admission for permanent residence, or

(B) a citizen parent of the citizen parent has been physically present in the United States or its outlying possessions for a period or periods totaling not less than five years, at least two of which were after the age of fourteen.

(b) Upon approval of the application (which may be filed abroad) and except as provided in the last sentence of section 337(a), upon taking and subscribing before an officer of the Service within the United States to the oath of allegiance required by this Act of an applicant for naturalization, the child shall become a citizen of the United

States and shall be furnished by the Attorney General with a certificate of citizenship.

(c) Subsection (a) of this section shall apply to the adopted child of a United States citizen adoptive parent if the conditions specified in such subsection have been fulfilled.

Former Citizens of the United States Regaining United States Citizenship.

Sec. 324. (U.S.C. 1435) (May 1995) (d)(1) A person who was a citizen of the United States at birth and lost such citizenship for failure to meet the physical presence retention requirements under section 301(b) (as in effect before October 10, 1978) shall, from and after taking the oath of allegiance required by section 337 be a citizen of the United States and have the status of a citizen of the United States by birth, without filing an application for naturalization, and notwithstanding any of the other provisions of section 313. Nothing in this subsection or any other provision of law shall be construed as conferring United States citizenship retroactively upon such person during any period in which such person was not a citizen.

Chapter 3—Loss of Nationality (May 1995)

Loss of Nationality by Native-born or Naturalized Citizens.

Sec. 349 (a) A person who is a national of the United States whether by birth or naturalization, shall lose his nationality by voluntarily performing any of the following acts with the intention of relinquishing United States nationality—

(1) obtaining naturalization in a foreign state upon his own application or upon an application filed by a duly authorized agent, after having attained the age of eighteen years; or

(4) (A) accepting, serving in, or performing the duties of any office, post, or employment under the government of a foreign state or a political subdivision thereof, after attaining the age of eighteen years if he has or acquires the nationality of such foreign state; or

(B) accepting, serving in, or performing the duties of any office, post, or employment under the government of a foreign state or a political subdivision thereof, after attaining the age of eighteen years for which office, post, or employment an oath, affirmation, or declaration of allegiance is required.

(b) Whenever the loss of United States nationality is put in issue in any action or proceeding commenced on or after the enactment of this subsection under, or by virture of, the provisions of this or any other Act, the burden shall be upon the person or party claiming that such loss occurred, to establish such claim by a preponderance of the evidence. Any person who commits, performs, or who has committed or performed, any act of expatriation under the provisions of this or any other Act shall be presumed to have done so voluntarily; but such presumption may be rebutted upon a showing, by a preponderance of the evidence, that the act or acts committed or performed were not done so voluntarily.

[Former subsection (b) was stricken by section 19 (1) of Public Law L 99-653, Nov. 14, 1986. It read as follows:

Any person who commits or performs any act specified in subsection (a) shall be conclusively presumed to have done so voluntarily and without having been subjected to duress of any kind, if such a person at the time of the act was a national of the state in which the act was performed and had been physically present in such state for a period or periods totaling ten years or more immediately prior to such act.]

The following shall be nationals and citizens of the United States at birth [in force between 1952 and 1968]:

Sec. 301 (a)(7)(7) a person born outside the geographicallimits of the United States and its outlying possessions of parents one of whom is an alien, and the other, a citizen of the United States who, prior to the birth of such person, was physically present in the United States or its outlying possessions for a period or periods totaling not less than ten years, at least five of which were after attaining the age of fourteen years: Provided, That any periods of honorable service in the Armed Forces of the United States or periods of employment with the United States Government or with an international organization as that term is defined in section 1 of the International Organizations Immunities Act (59 Stat. 669; 22 U.S.C. 288) by such citizen parent or any periods during which such citizen is physically present abroad as the dependent unmarried son or daughter and a member of the household of a person

(A) honorably serving with the Armed Forces of the United States, or

(B) employed by the United States Government or an international organization as defined in section 1 of the International Organizations Immunities Act, may be included in order to satisfy the physical-presence requirement of this paragraph.

(b) Any person who is a national or citizen of the United States at birth under paragraph (7) of subsection (a), shall lose his nationality and citizenship unless he shall come to the United States prior to attaining the age of twenty-three years and shall immediately following any such coming be continuously physically present in the United States for at least five years: Provided, That such physical presence follows the attainment of the age of fourteen years and precedes the age of twenty-eight years.

Public Law 92-584, 92nd Congress H.R. 8273, October 27, 1972, Section 301(b) is amended to read as follows:

(b) Any person who is a national and citizen of the United States under paragraph (7) of subsection (a) shall lose his nationality and citizenship unless—(1) he shall come to the United States and be continuously physically present therein for a period of not less than two years between the ages of fourteen years and twenty-eight years;

Public Law 95-432, October 10, 1978, repealed subsection (b), thus eliminating the residence requirement for retention of United States citizenship. This change was effective on October 10, 1978, and is prospective in nature (viz., it does not reinstate as citizens those who had lost citizenship under section 301(b) as previous in effect).

Bibliography

American Citizens Abroad, *A Handbook for Citizens Living Abroad* (New York: Doubleday, 1990).

Atwell, Judith, *AARO, The First Ten Years, 1973–1983* (Paris: Association of American Residents Overseas, 1983).

Bainbridge, John, *Another Way of Living: A Gallery of Americans Who Choose to Live in Europe* (New York: Holt, Rinehart & Winston, 1968).

Boutin, Alexandra, and Carolyn White-Lesieur (eds.), *AAWE Living in France* (Paris: Association of American Wives of Europeans, 1993).

Cleveland, Harlan, Gerald J. Mangone, and John Clark Adams, *The Overseas Americans* (New York: McGraw-Hill, 1960).

de Klerk-Rubin, V. (ed.), *American Women & Work Overseas* (Paris: Federation of American Women's Clubs Overseas, 1992).

Dulles, Rhea Foster, *Americans Abroad: Two Centuries of European Travel* (Ann Arbor: University of Michigan Press, 1964).

Fabre, Katheryn, Tara Whitbeck, and Carolyn White-Lesieur (eds.), *AAWE Guide to Education* (Paris: Association of American Wives of Europeans, 1995).

Hootsmans, Helen, and Longina Jakibowska, *Female Globetrotters, Undervalued Team Members of the GNP* (American Women's Club of The Hague, 1995).

Metraux, Ruth W., "A Study of Bilingualism Among Children of U.S.-French Parents," *The French Review,* vol. 38, no. 5.

Staudt, J., and others, *Handbook for the American Family Abroad* (American Women's Club of Luxembourg, 1989).

Varro, Gabrielle, "Couples franco-américains en France: génèse et devenir d'une mixité," in *Mariages mixtes, Hommes et Migrations* (July 1993).

Varro, Gabrielle, *The Transplanted Woman: A Study of French American Marriages in France* (New York: Praeger, 1988) (*La Femme Transplantée: Une étude du mariage franco-américain en France et le bilinguisme des enfants,* Presses Universitaires de Lille, 1984).

Index